WOHNEN IN REIZVOLLER UMGEBUNG
HOUSES IN SPECTACULAR SETTINGS
MAISONS DE RÊVE EN TERRE SAUVAGE
HUIZEN OP OPVALLENDE LOCATIES

WOHNEN IN REIZVOLLER UMGEBUNG

HOUSES IN SPECTACULAR SETTINGS

MAISONS DE RÊVE EN TERRE SAUVAGE

HUIZEN OP OPVALLENDE LOCATIES

FKG

FKG

Editorial project:
2008 © **LOFT Publications**
Via Laietana, 32, 4.º, Of. 92
08003 Barcelona, Spain
Tel.: +34 932 688 088
Fax: +34 932 687 073
loft@loftpublications.com
www.loftpublications.com

Art director:
Mireia Casanovas Soley

Editorial coordination:
Simone Schleifer

Editor:
Cristina Paredes

Texts:
LOFT Publications

Layout:
Print Plate

Translations coordination:
Equipo de Edición, Barcelona
Translations: Katrin Kügler (German), Éditions 360 (French),
Persklaar (Dutch)

ISBN 978-84-96936-82-9

Printed in China

Einleitung

In den letzten Jahren haben Kommunikationstechnologie und moderne Transportmittel unseren Lebensstil entscheidend verändert – davon blieb der Begriff des idealen Heims nicht unberührt. Ferienhäuser werden zum Erstwohnsitz, Häuser in den Bergen oder an der Küste verwandeln sich in Ateliers oder Büros. Wohnhäuser müssen an die unterschiedlichsten topografischen, klimatischen und geologischen Gegebenheiten angepasst werden. Dazu kommen die nicht selten unkonventionellen Vorstellungen der Bewohner. Dazu spielt die Beschaffenheit des Grundstücks beim Grundriss, der Platzierung der Fenster und bei der Gestaltung bis hin zum Eingangsbereich eine maßgebliche Rolle.

Introduction

In recent years improvements in communications and transport have changed people's lifestyles and thus the concept of the home has been revised. Holiday homes have become first homes and houses in the mountains or on the coast can easily be transformed into studios or offices. Every type of topographic, climatic, geological and other features has come into play in order to adapt the dwellings to the owner's wishes. The projects vary according to their requirements, and there are countless ways the layout of the bedrooms and living areas may differ from a conventional layout. As well as a change in concept, the lots may influence the layout of the rooms on each floor, the openings to the exterior and even access to the dwellings.

Introduction

Ces dernières années, l'évolution des moyens de communication et des transports a transformé les modes de vie et, par conséquent, le concept même de la maison. Les maisons de vacances sont devenues des résidences principales qui se transforment aisément en atelier ou en bureau, que ce soit à la montagne ou en bord de mer. Chaque caractéristique topographique, climatique, géologique doit être prise en considération afin de s'adapter au désir du propriétaire. L'agencement des chambres et des pièces à vivre peut varier et s'éloigner de la distribution classique. Le terrain n'influence pas seulement la conception, mais aussi la disposition des pièces à chaque étage, les ouvertures et l'accès à l'habitation.

Inleiding

In de afgelopen jaren is onze levensstijl door verbeterde communicatie- en vervoermiddelen veranderd, en daarmee is ook het concept van de woning herzien. Vakantiehuizen zijn eerste huizen geworden en van huizen in de bergen of aan de kust kan een werkruimte worden gemaakt. Elk kenmerk, of dit nu topografisch, klimatologisch of geologisch is, speelt een rol wanneer een huis aan de wensen van de eigenaar wordt aangepast. Er zijn talloze mogelijkheden om een slaap- of woonkamer te laten afwijken van een traditionele indeling. Net als de verandering van het woningconcept kunnen de percelen de indeling van de kamers en verdiepingen, de openingen naar buiten en zelfs de toegang van het huis beïnvloeden.

WOHNEN IN REIZVOLLER UMGEBUNG
HOUSES IN SPECTACULAR SETTINGS
MAISONS DE RÊVE EN TERRE SAUVAGE
HUIZEN OP OPVALLENDE LOCATIES

RESIDENCE 104

Miró Rivera

Austin, TX, U.S.A. | 2004
Photographs © Paul Bardagjy

Bei diesem sehr hoch gelegenen Gebäude wurde eine großzügige Fläche für den Aufenthalt im Freien einkalkuliert und der Wohnraum so gestaltet, dass die spektakuläre Aussicht auf den Lake Austin, das Colorado Valley und das umliegende Bergland bewundert werden kann.

As with most houses on high ground, the architects were faced with the challenge of creating a large area for the exterior spaces and siting the dwelling to look over the impressive views of Lake Austin, the Colorado Valley and the Hill Country beyond.

Comme pour la plupart des maisons situées en hauteur, les architectes ont dû relever le défi de créer de grandes surfaces externes et de situer la maison de telle sorte qu'elle bénéficie de la vue impressionnante sur le lac Austin, la vallée du Colorado et jusqu'à la région de Hill Country.

Zoals bij de meeste hooggelegen huizen zagen de architecten zich voor de uitdaging gesteld het accent op de oriëntatie naar buiten te leggen en het huis zo te situeren dat het een indrukwekkend uitzicht had over het Austinmeer, de Coloradovallei en de Hill Country erachter.

Der Wohnbereich wurde durch einen Verbindungs-durchgang beider Gebäudeteile vergrößert.

A breezeway connecting two areas of the lot has provided extra space for this residence.

La galerie, en reliant deux parcelles du terrain, donne de l'espace à cette résidence.

Een overdekte passage verbindt de twee zones van het perceel en biedt de woning extra ruimte.

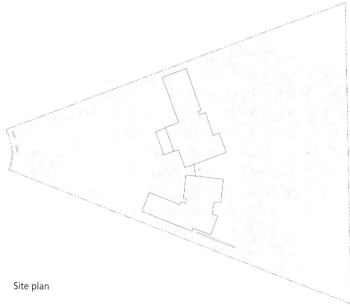

Site plan

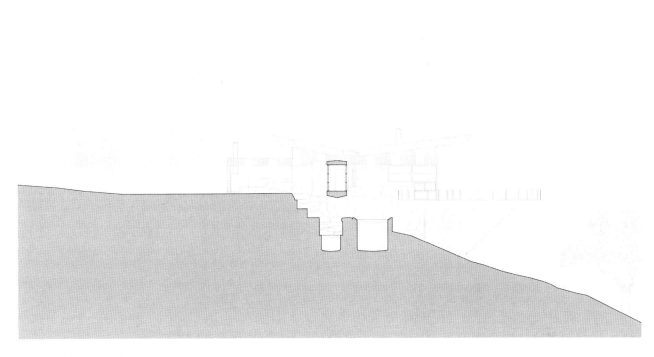

Section of the bridge facing west

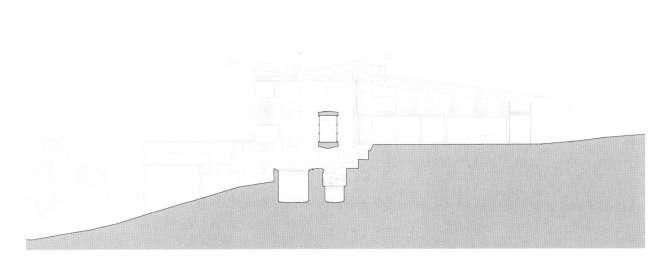

Section of the bridge facing east

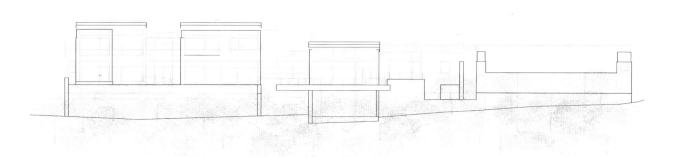

North elevation

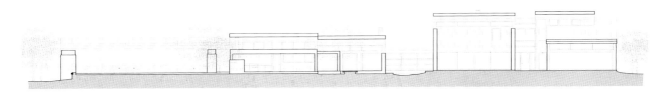

South elevation

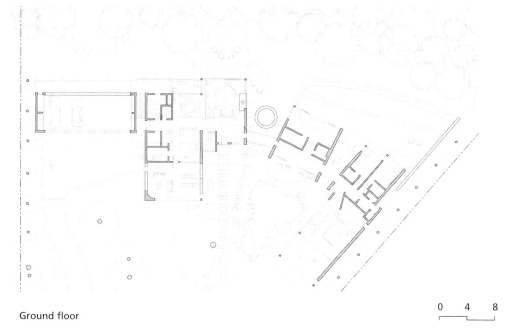

Ground floor

0   4   8

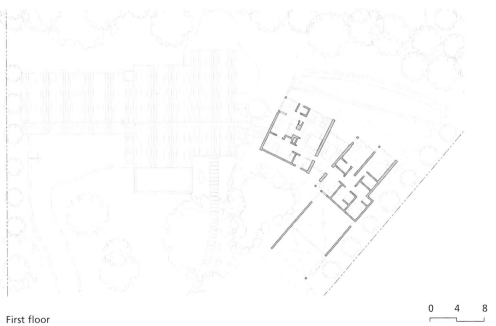

First floor

0   4   8

CASA XSMC

Estudi d'Arquitectura Set

Port de la Selva, Girona, Spain | 2005
Photographs © Eugeni Pons

Dieses Wohnhaus liegt in einem kleinen katalanischen Ort an der Costa Brava, dessen Bewohner von Fischfang und Tourismus leben. Schlichte Eleganz zeichnet dieses Gebäude aus – sie zeigt sich in der Aufteilung der Räume, der Beschaffenheit der Materialien und einen besonderen Stil.

This residence is to be found on the Catalonian coast in a small community on the Costa Brava the main activities of which are fishing and tourism. Discretion is one of the features of this building, to be seen in the size of the rooms, the quality of the finishings and its own particular style.

Elle se situe sur la côte catalane, non loin d'une petite ville de la Costa Brava vivant essentiellement de la pêche et du tourisme. La discrétion est l'une des caractéristiques de cette construction, comme le montre le choix de la taille des pièces, la qualité des finitions et son style très personnel.

Deze woning is te vinden aan de kust van Catalonië, in een dorpje aan de Costa Brava waar visserij en toerisme de belangrijkste bestaansmiddelen zijn. Het gebouw is stijlvol en elegant vormgegeven, met een goede ruimte-indeling en fraaie afwerkingen.

Dieses Wohnhaus wurde auf schwer bebaubarem abschüssigem Gelände errichtet.

The residence has been built on a complex lot, with a steep slope.

La résidence a été construite sur un terrain difficile, car très pentu.

De woning is gebouwd op moeilijk terrein met een steile helling.

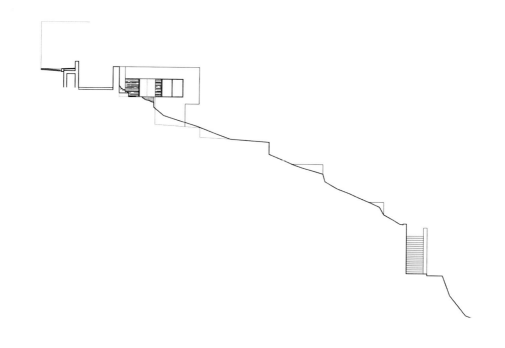

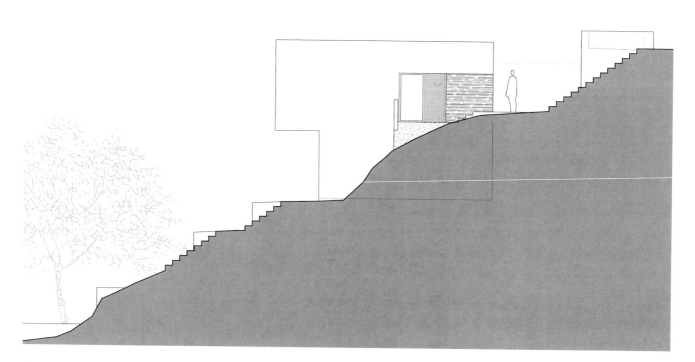

Elevations

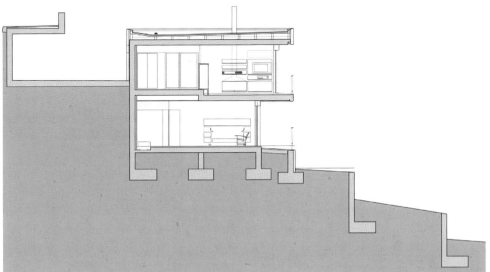

Section

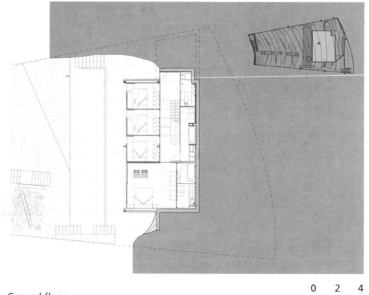

Ground floor

0   2   4

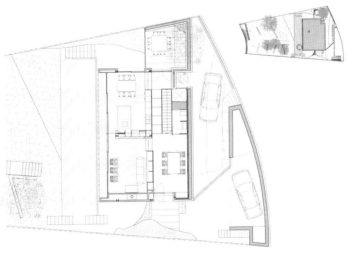

First floor

0 2 4

KATSUURA VILLA

Chiba Manabu Architects

Katsuura, Chiba, Japan | 2003
Photographs © Nacása & Partners

Ein Kontrast entsteht zwischen dem Minimalismus des Bauwerks und der Komplexität der Innenräume. Die Grundfläche des auf einem 575 m² großen Grundstück errichteten Hauses beträgt 70 m². Man genießt den Ausblick auf das Meer, die Hügel, den Wald und ein Fischerdorf.

The minimalist geometry of the structure contrasts with the complexity of the interior spaces. This residence occupies an area of 750 sq ft on a lot measuring some 6,200 sq ft. From the top of the hill there are views of the ocean, the hills, the forest and the fishing village on the coast.

La géométrie minimaliste de sa structure contraste avec la sophistication de ses espaces intérieurs. Cette maison occupe 70 m² sur un terrain d'environ 575 m². Du haut de la colline, on découvre l'océan, les collines environnantes, la forêt et le village de pêcheurs.

De minimalistische geometrie van het bouwwerk contrasteert met de complexe binnenruimten. De woning beslaat een gebied van 70 m² op een stuk grond van 575 m². Vanaf de top van de heuvel is er uitzicht over de oceaan, de heuvels, het bos en het vissersdorp aan de kust.

Die auf einem Hügel errichtete Villa liegt in der Nähe eines Fischerdorfes.

This villa has been built at the top of a hill near a fishing village.

Cette villa a été bâtie au sommet d'une colline près d'un village de pêcheurs.

Deze villa is gebouwd op een heuveltop dicht bij een vissersdorp.

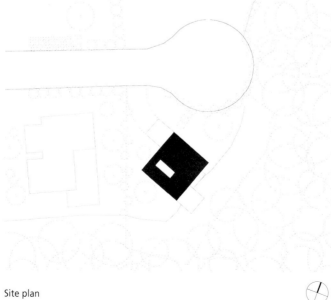

Site plan

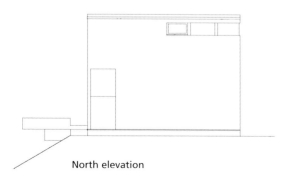

North elevation

East elevation

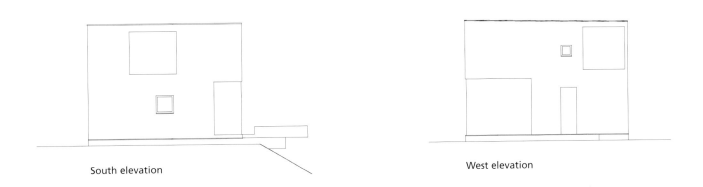

South elevation

West elevation

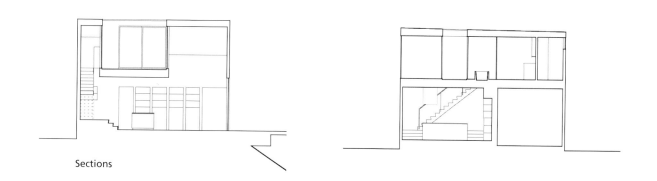

Sections

Ground floor

First floor

0 1 2

GARCÍA RESIDENCE

Ibarra Rosano
Design Architects

Tucson, AZ, U.S.A. | 2001
Photographs © Bill Timmerman

Die südliche Arizona-Wüste ist eine der beeindruckendsten Regionen der Welt, besonders während der sommerlichen Regenzeit. Die einfachen, widerstandsfähigen Materialien dieses Wohnhauses eignen sich für die klimatischen Bedingungen und fügen sich perfekt in die Umgebung ein.

The southern Arizona desert is one of the most dramatic regions in the world, particularly during the wet season in summer, when there are extremely spectacular rain and electrical storms. The range of materials is simple, long-lasting and sensitive to the desert climate, its colors and textures.

Le désert du sud de l'Arizona est une des régions les plus spectaculaires au monde, notamment lors de la saison humide, en été, quand le ciel est chargé de pluie et illuminé d'éclairs. La gamme des matériaux choisis est simple, résistante et influencée par le climat du désert, tant pour les couleurs et que pour les textures.

Het zuiden van de Arizonawoestijn is een van de imposantste streken ter wereld, vooral tijdens het regenseizoen 's zomers. Er zijn dan spectaculaire regen- en onweersbuien. De materialen zijn eenvoudig, duurzaam en afgestemd op het klimaat, de kleuren en structuren van de woestijn.

Dieses Grundstück befindet sich an einem Nordhang in den Ausläufern der Tucson Mountains.

The lot is on a north-facing slope in the foothills of Mount Tucson.

Ce terrain se trouve sur le versant nord des contreforts du mont Lemmon, près de Tucson.

Het perceel bevindt zich aan de voet van Mount Tucson op de noordelijke helling.

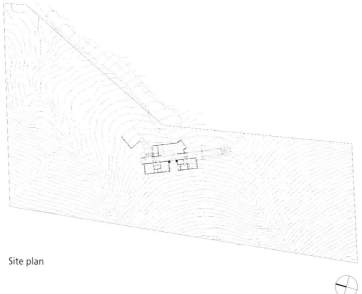

Site plan

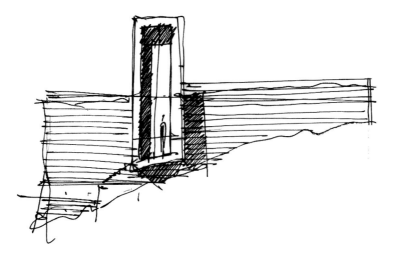

Sketch

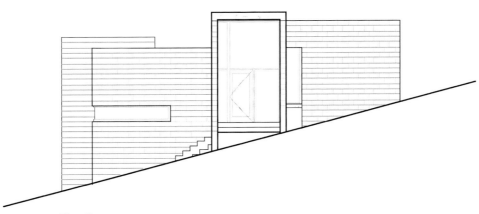

Elevation

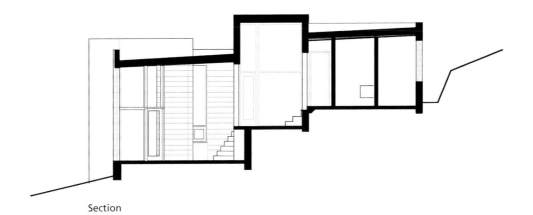

Section

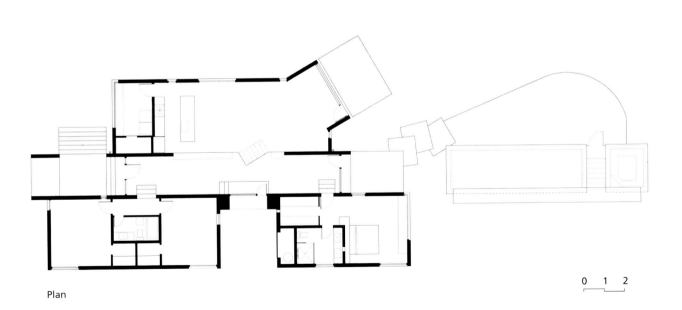

Plan

0 1 2

POLI HOUSE

Pezo von Ellrichshausen Arquitectos

Coliumo Peninsula, Chile | 2005
Photographs © Cristobal Palma

Ein beschauliches Fleckchen Land bildet den Sitz dieses Wohnhauses. Um die Idylle nicht zu zerstören, wurde ein schlichtes kompaktes Gebäude entworfen und vom Ufer leicht zurückversetzt situiert. Als Baumaterial wurde hauptsächlich verputzter Beton mit rauer Optik verwendet.

The land where the dwelling was to be built is an idyllic spot. Faced by the fact that the house might spoil it, the architects decided to create a plain, compact structure, situated a little way back from the shore. The material used was basically rough-finished concrete.

Le terrain sur lequel cette maison devait être construite est un lieu idyllique. Conscients qu'une construction pourrait en rompre l'harmonie, les architectes décidèrent de créer une structure simple et compacte, légèrement en recul par rapport à la côte et réalisée essentiellement en béton brut.

De plek waar de woning gebouwd moest worden, was heel idyllisch. Omdat het huis de omgeving kon bederven, besloten de architecten een eenvoudig, compact bouwwerk te maken dat iets van de kust af stond. Het gebruikte materiaal is in hoofdzaak ruw afgewerkt beton.

Das „Poli House" steht majestätisch auf einer Klippe mit Ausblick aufs Meer.

The Poli House stands majestically on top of a cliff overlooking the ocean.

La maison Poli se dresse majestueusement sur une falaise, face à l'océan.

Huis Poli staat majestueus boven op een steile rots en ziet uit over de oceaan.

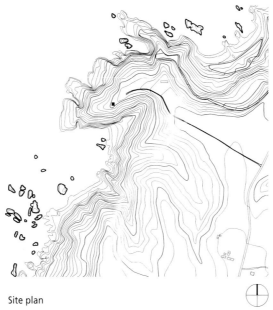

Site plan

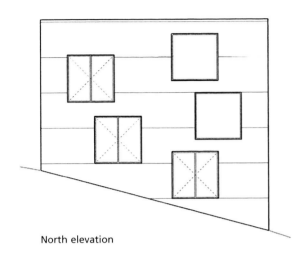

North elevation

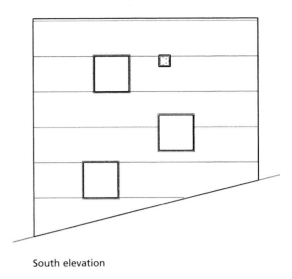

South elevation

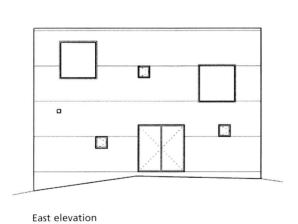

East elevation

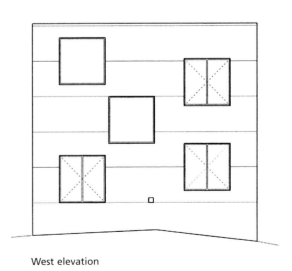

West elevation

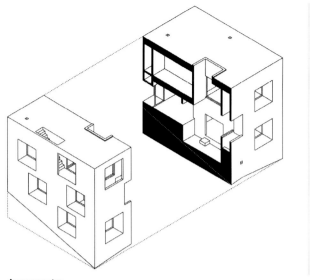

Axonometry

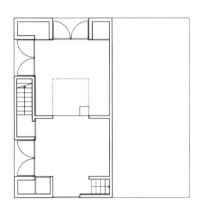

Ground floor

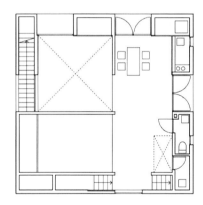

First floor

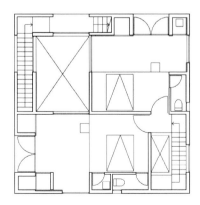

Second floor

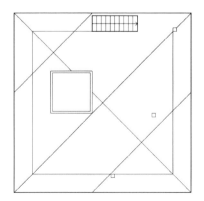

Roof plan

0   1   2

MOUNTAIN CABIN IN HEMSEDAL

Div.A Arkitekter

Hemsedal, Norway | 2005
Photographs © Div.A Arkitekter, Michael Perlmutter

Ein Skigebiet, in dem in jüngster Zeit zahlreiche Ferien und Freizeitgebäude errichtet wurden, liegt in unmittelbarer Nähe zu dem an einem Hang gelegenen Grundstück. Aufgrund des leichten Gefälles besteht das einstöckige Gebäude aus zwei in unterschiedlicher Höhe gelegenen Ebenen.

In the area where this residence stands, on a hillside very near a ski resort, various leisure buildings have recently been put up. This means that one can get to the pistes on skis. The house stands on a gentle slope which has been resolved by building it on two levels.

À proximité de la résidence se trouve une station de ski. Les pistes sont directement accessibles depuis la maison. Comme le terrain était légèrement en pente, il a fallu construire sur deux niveaux.

In het gebied waar deze woning staat, op een heuvel dicht bij een skiresort, werd recentelijk een aantal vrijetijdscentra gebouwd. Daardoor kunnen mensen op hun ski's de piste bereiken. Het probleem dat het huis op een lichte helling staat, is opgelost door het twee verdiepingen te geven.

Das Design unterscheidet klar zwischen Wohnbereich und Schlaf bzw. Badezimmern.

The design of this residence makes a clear distinction between private and living areas.

Chambres et pièces à vivre sont clairement séparées dès la conception.

Het ontwerp van deze woning maakt duidelijk onderscheid tussen de woon- en privévertrekken.

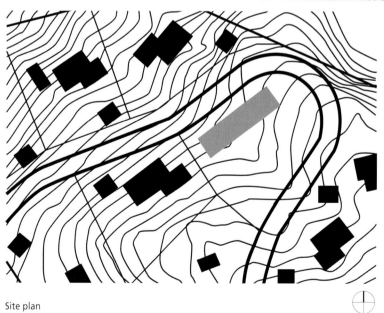

Site plan

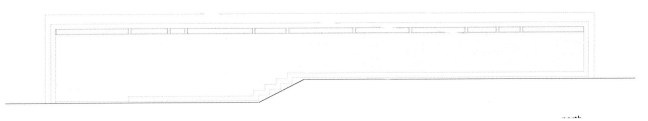

North elevation

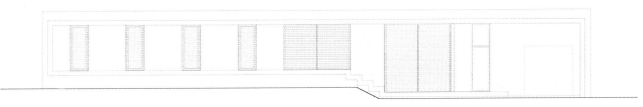

South elevation

East elevation

West elevation

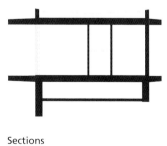

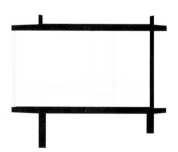

Sections

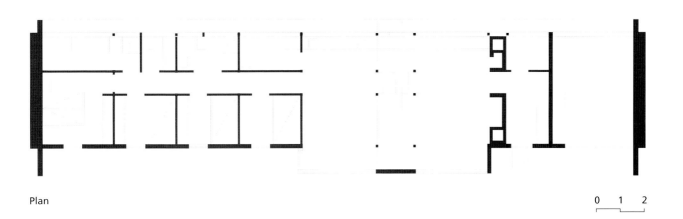

Plan

0   1   2

HOUSE IN VALLVIDRERA

Francisco de la Guardia

Vallvidrera, Barcelona, Spain | 2000
Photographs © Jordi Miralles

Das extreme Gefälle des Baugrundstücks bestimmte maßgeblich die Konstruktion dieses Bauwerks. Es besteht aus drei Einzelbauten auf verschiedenen Ebenen. So wird die spektakuläre Aussicht auf die Stadt ermöglicht und gleichzeitig das Haus an das komplexe Grundstücks angepasst.

The extreme unevenness of the lot is the element that has determined how this dwelling has been built. In order to make the most of the views over the city, three structures were built on different levels, and this resolved the question of adapting the house to the lot.

L'irrégularité du terrain a été un élément déterminant dans la construction de cette demeure. Afin de profiter au maximum de la vue sur la ville, trois structures ont été construites à différents niveaux, résolvant ainsi les problèmes d'adaptation au terrain.

Het extreem onregelmatige terrein was bepalend voor de manier waarop het huis gebouwd werd. Om vooral uitzicht op de stad te hebben, werden drie gedeelten op verschillend niveau gebouwd. Zo werd het probleem opgelost van hoe het bouwwerk aan het terrein moest worden aangepast.

Der steile Hang bietet eine herrliche Aussicht auf die katalanische Hauptstadt.

This house has been built on a steeply-sloping hillside with magnificent views of Barcelona.

Cette maison construite sur une colline escarpée dispose d'une vue magnifique sur Barcelone.

Dit huis is gebouwd op de steile helling van een heuvel met schitterend uitzicht op Barcelona.

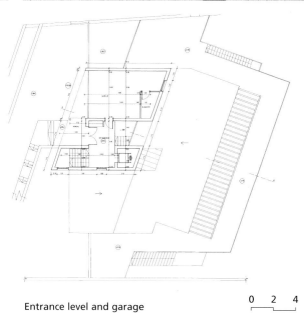

Entrance level and garage

0   2   4

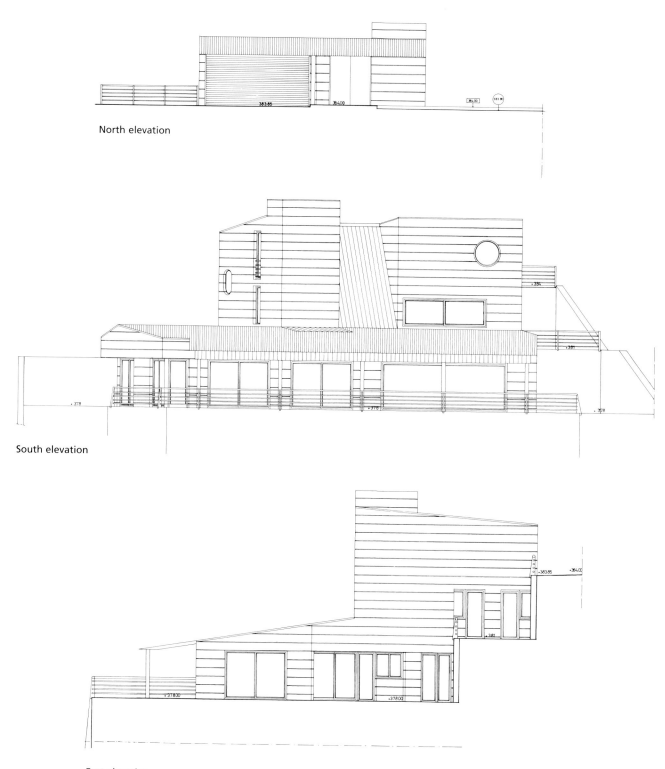

North elevation

South elevation

East elevation

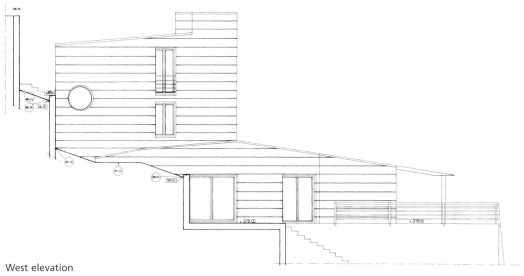

West elevation

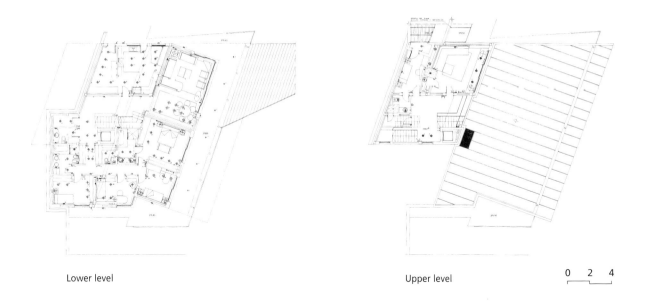

Lower level

Upper level

0   2   4

CASA TÓLÓ

Álvaro Leite Siza Vieira

Lugar das Carvalhinhas, Alvite, Portugal | 2005
Photographs © Fernando Guerra/FG+SG

Dank seiner Südlage sind die Räume dieses Hauses, das sich über einen Hang mit 35-Grad-Gefälle erstreckt, von Sonnenlicht durchflutet. Aufgrund des Höhenunterschieds wurde der Gesamtbau auf mehrere miteinander verbundene, auf verschiedenen Ebenen liegende Gebäude verrteilt.

This house has been built on a small lot in the north of the country. Its elongated, narrow shape is marked by a 35-degree slope. The pronounced slope of the lot is the reason for the breaking up of the spaces into different structures, one of the most striking features of this project.

Cette habitation a été construite sur une petite parcelle, dans le nord du pays. Sa forme allongée et étroite est marquée par une pente à 35 degrés. Cette forte inclinaison explique le morcellement en plusieurs structures, ce qui constitue l'un des aspects les plus étonnants de ce projet.

Dit huis is gebouwd op een klein perceel in het noorden van het land. De langwerpige, smalle vorm heeft een helling van 35 graden. De sterke helling is de reden dat de ruimte werd uitgesplitst over verschillende bouwvolumes, een van de opvallendste kenmerken van het ontwerp.

Ein kleines Grundstück im Norden des Landes bildet den Baugrund für dieses Haus.

Its southern orientation enables it to receive lots of sunlight.

Exposée au sud, cette maison bénéficie d'un ensoleillement maximal.

Door de ligging op het zuiden krijgt het huis veel zonlicht.

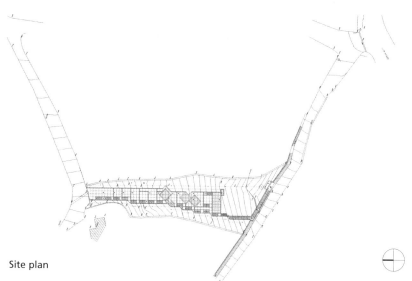

Site plan

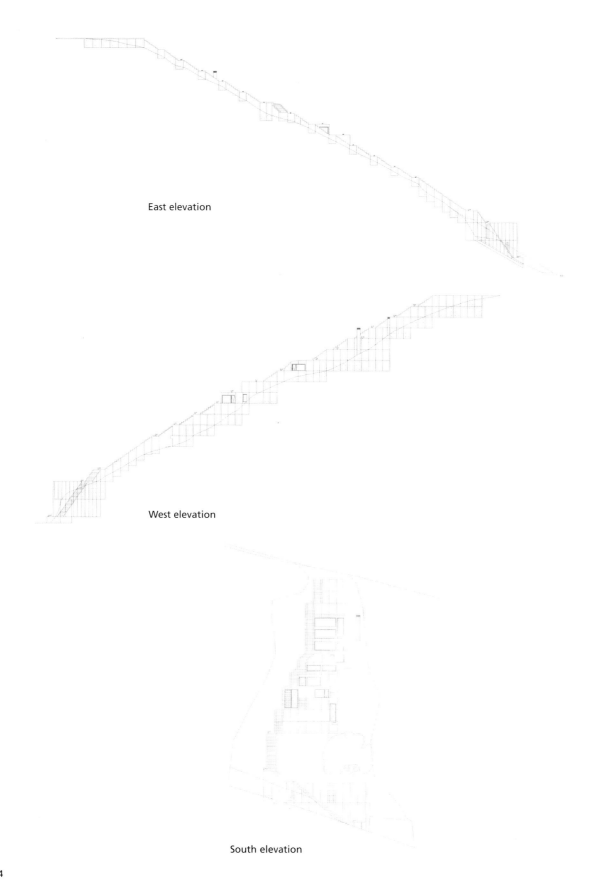

East elevation

West elevation

South elevation

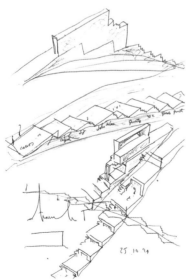

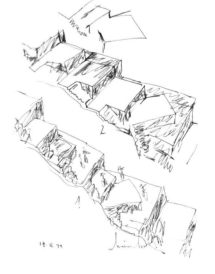

Sketches

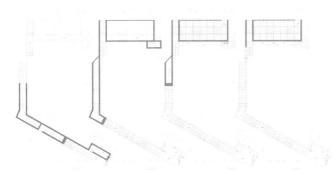

Floor plan level -7 to -4

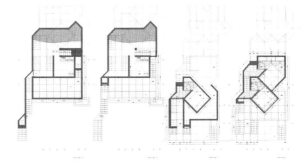

Floor plan level -3 to 0

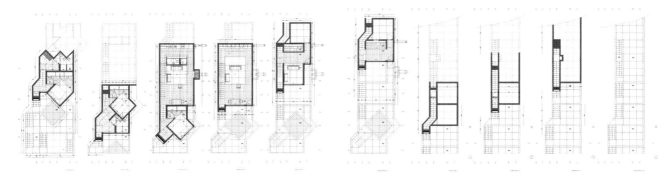

Floor plan level 1 to 5

Floor plan level 6 to 9

0   4   8

HILL HOUSE

Johnston Marklee & Associates

Pacific Palisades, CA, U.S.A. | 2004
Photographs © Eric Staudenmaier

Mehrere Probleme mussten hier gelöst werden: Auf einem kleinen, unregelmäßigen Baugrund sollte unter Einhaltung strenger Baubestimmungen ein großzügiges Haus mit Blick auf den Santa Monica Canyon errichtet werden, ohne den Charakter des bewachsenen Hügels zu zerstören.

This residence is a response to the challenge to build a spacious dwelling with views of Santa Monica Canyon on a small irregular lot, and also having to comply with some rigorous building regulations. It was also necessary to preserve the natural profile of the hillside.

Le cahier des charges de cette habitation était le suivant : bâtir une demeure spacieuse avec vue sur le canyon de Santa Monica, sur une parcelle petite et irrégulière, tout en respectant la réglementation et en préservant l'environnement naturel.

Deze woning is het antwoord op de uitdaging een ruime woning te bouwen met uitzicht op Santa Monica Canyon, op een klein, onregelmatig stuk grond. Daarbij moest een aantal strenge bouwregels worden nageleefd. Ook moest het natuurlijke aanzien van de heuvel bewaard blijven.

Strenge Bauvorschriften machten dieses Bauprojekt in Hanglage zu einer Herausforderung.

The numerous strict building regulations made this building on a slope a challenge.

La stricte réglementation des permis de construire a constitué un défi pour la conception de cette villa.

Door de vele strenge bouwreglementen vormde dit gebouw op een helling een echte uitdaging.

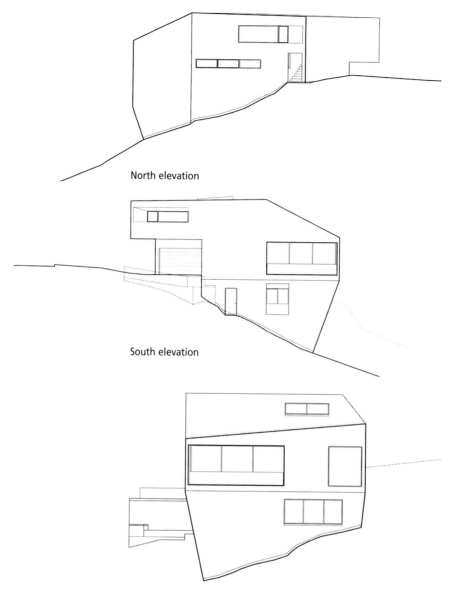

North elevation

South elevation

East elevation

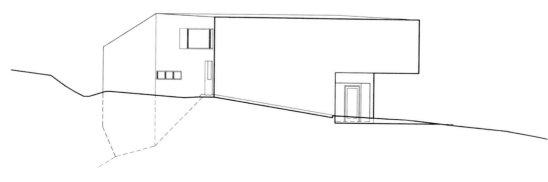

West elevation

Axonometries

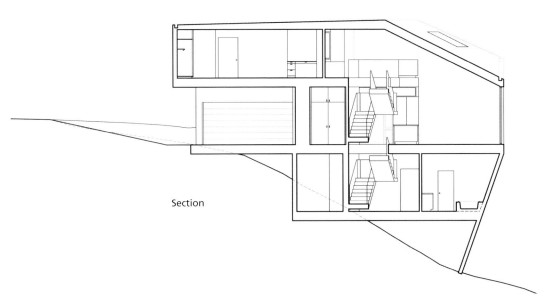

Section

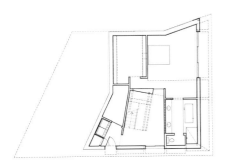

Ground floor

First floor

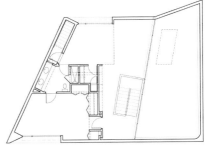

Second floor

0 1 2

VILLA IN THE SOUTH OF FRANCE

Atelier Barani

France | 2004
Photographs © Serge Demailly

Auf der Spitze eines am Mittelmeer gelegenen Hügels errichtet, verfügt dieses Sommerhaus über eine minimalistische Bauweise, die sich besonders gut in die Landschaft einfügt. Hier wurde die französische Tradition fortgesetzt, den Sommer in einem Ferienhaus im Süden des Landes zu verbringen.

Situated on top of a hill with spectacular views of the Mediterranean, this summer residence shows light, minimalist lines which create a particular way of experiencing the landscape. This project was built to follow the long-standing tradition of spending the summer in the South of France.

Située au sommet d'une colline avec une vue spectaculaire sur la Méditerranée, cette résidence d'été présente des lignes délicates et épurées qui permettent d'appréhender le paysage environnant avec une perspective inhabituelle.

Dit zomerverblijf, op een heuveltop met uitzicht over de Middellandse Zee, heeft lichte, minimalistische lijnen die ervoor zorgen dat het landschap op een bijzondere manier ervaren wordt. Het huis werd gebouwd in navolging van de traditie om de zomer in Zuid-Frankrijk door te brengen.

Dieses Grundstück mit Meerblick wird ganzen Tag über mit Sonnenlicht versorgt.

The lot is on a slope and faces the sea and the course of the sun.

Ce terrain en pente fait face à la mer et à la course du soleil.

Het perceel ligt op een helling en ziet uit op de zee en de baan die de zon beschrijft.

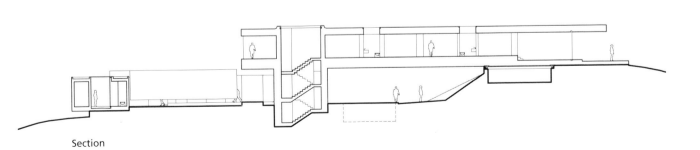

Section

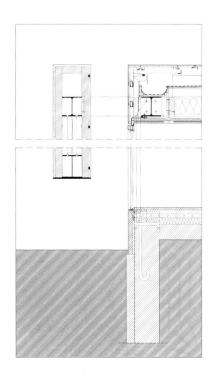

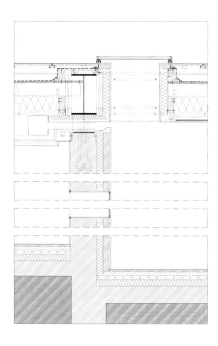

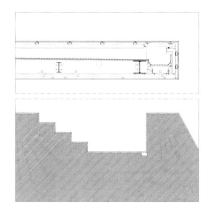

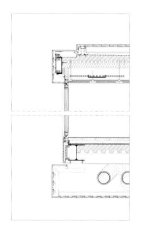

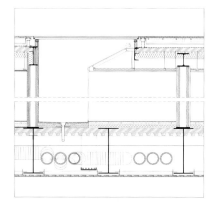

Construction details

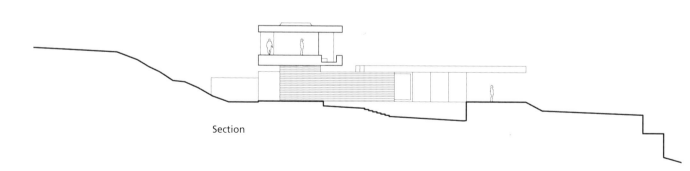

Section

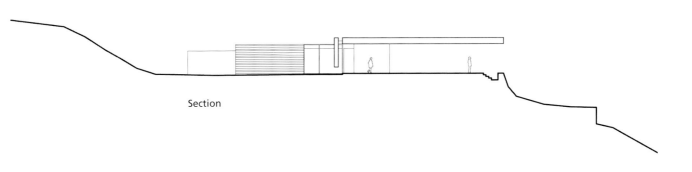

Section

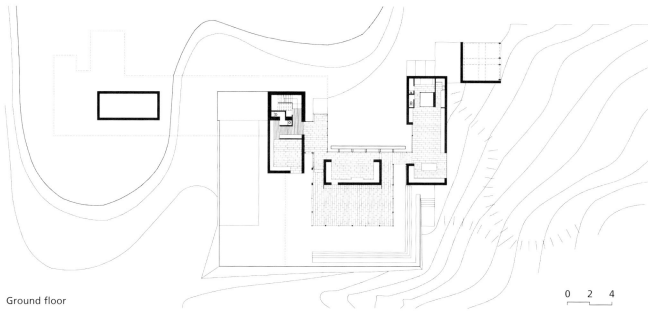

Ground floor

0   2   4

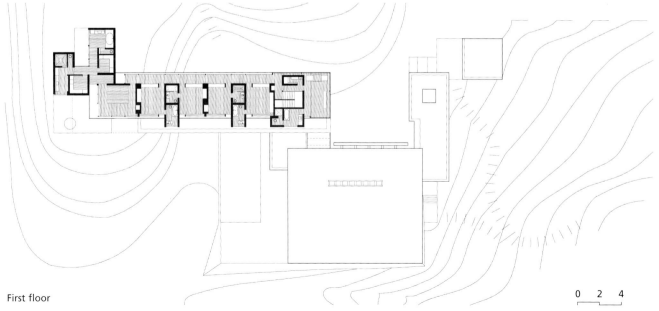

First floor

HOUSE IN MALIBU

Kanner Architects

Malibu, CA, U.S.A. | 2004
Photographs © John Linden

Dieses Haus, ein Paradebeispiel für die moderne kalifornische Architektur, besteht aus zwei Kuben, die durch eine Treppe miteinander verbunden werden. Ein reizvoller Kontrast entsteht durch die schlichten, gradlinigen Formen vor einer zerklüfteten hügeligen Landschaft.

This building is an example of modern Californian architecture. The residence is essentially two cubes linked by a staircase. The simplicity of its lines contrasts with the wild craggy landscape of the surrounding hills.

Exemple type de l'architecture moderne californienne, cette résidence consiste essentiellement en deux cubes reliés par un escalier. La simplicité des lignes contraste avec le paysage sauvage et escarpé des collines environnantes.

Het gebouw is een voorbeeld van moderne Californische architectuur. De woning bestaat in feite uit twee door een trap met elkaar verbonden blokken. De eenvoud van de lijnen contrasteert met het wilde, ruwe landschap van de omliggende heuvels.

Dieses Gebäude befindet sich an der Stelle des durch ein Feuer zerstörten ursprünglichen Wohnhauses.

This house stands where, ten years previously, the owner lost his home because of a fire.

Cette villa a été construite à l'endroit où brûla, dix ans plus tôt, la précédente demeure du propriétaire.

Dit huis staat op de plek waar de eigenaar tien jaar eerder zijn huis door brand kwijtraakte.

Site plan

North elevation

South elevation

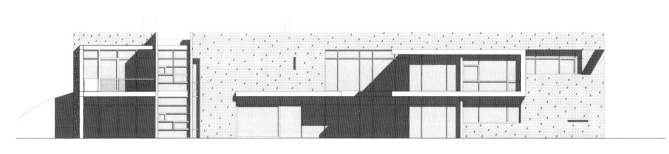

East elevation

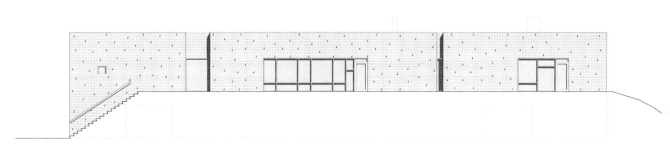

West elevation

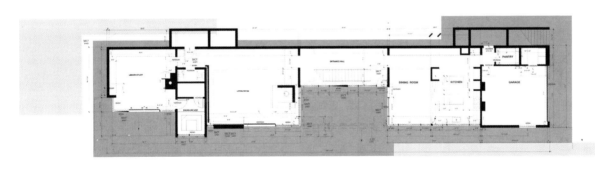

Ground floor

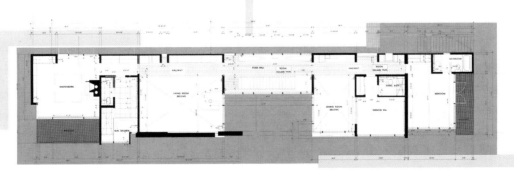

First floor

0 1 2

AGOSTA HOUSE

Patkau Architects

San Juan Island, WA, U.S.A. | 2000
Photographs © James Dow/Patkau Architects

Etwa 17 Hektar umfasst das von Pinien und Tannenwald bedeckte Grundstück. Es liegt auf San Juan Island, in der Meerenge von Georgia im US-Bundesstaat Washington. Das in Grasland eingebettete Haus bildet eine Art Grenze, die das Grundstück in zwei Bereiche einteilt.

The property consists of a 43-acre lot largely covered by a pine and fir tree forest. It is sited on San Juan Island, one of the islands in the Strait of Georgia, in Washington State. The house is laid out on the grassland and forms a sort of barrier dividing the space.

La propriété couvre plus de 17 hectares de forêt de pins et de sapins. Elle se trouve sur l'île San Juan, dans le détroit de Géorgie (État de Washington). La maison est située dans la prairie et fait ainsi office de barrière divisant l'espace.

Dit stuk grond van 17 hectare is grotendeels begroeid met pijnbomen en sparren. Het is gelegen op San Juan Island, een van de eilanden in de Straat van Georgia in de staat Washington. Het huis is op grasland gebouwd en rijst op als een soort barrière die de ruimte verdeelt.

Dichter Wald umgibt das auf einer Hügelkuppe errichtete Gebäude.

The house stands on the brow of a hill and is surrounded by a thick fir tree forest.

La maison se dresse au sommet d'une colline, entourée d'une forêt dense.

Het huis staat op een heuvelkam en wordt omgeven door een dicht naaldwoud.

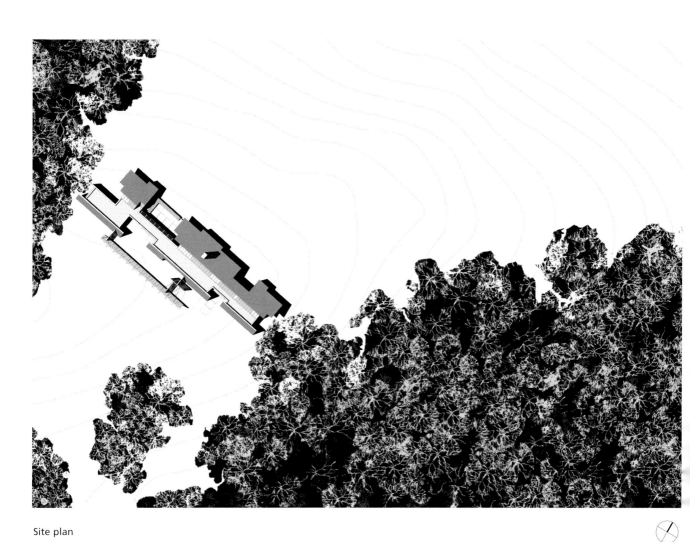

Site plan

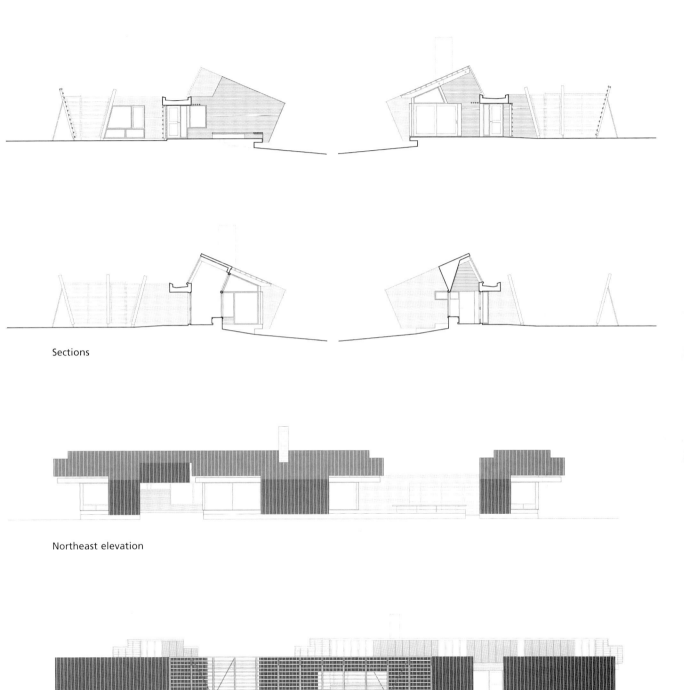

Sections

Northeast elevation

Southwest elevation

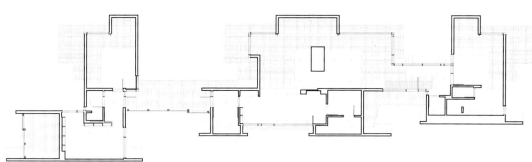

Reflected ceiling plan

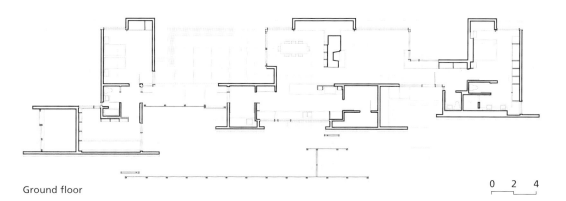

Ground floor

0   2   4

VINEYARD RESIDENCE

John Wardle Architects

Victoria, Australia | 2004
Photographs © Trevor Mein

Der unregelmäßige, parallel zu den Weinstöcken verlaufende Grundriss sorgt für eine visuelle Spannung, die dem Gebäude Dynamik verleiht. Bei der Gestaltung des Wohnhauses wurde außerdem darauf geachtet, dass der Blick auf die Weinberge uneingeschränkt möglich bleibt.

The design of this home has a floor plan laid out parallel with the lines of vines and its irregular shape creates a visual tension that provides the structure with dynamism. The structure is also orientated to take full advantage of views of the vineyards.

Le plan du sol de cette maison est parallèle aux rangées de vignes, tandis que sa forme irrégulière crée une tension visuelle dynamique. Elle est également orientée de manière à pouvoir profiter au maximum de la vue sur le vignoble.

De bouwtekening van dit ontwerp loopt parallel met de lijnen van de wijnstokken, terwijl de onregelmatige vorm voor een visuele spanning zorgt die het bouwwerk dynamiek geeft. Het huis is zo gelegen dat het optimaal geniet van het uitzicht over de wijngaarden.

Der Eigentümer verlegte seinen Wohnsitz in das in einem Weinberg gelegene Bauwerk.

This house is located in a vineyard and responds to the owner's wish to move to the country.

Située dans un vignoble, cette maison incarne le rêve de son propriétaire : vivre à la campagne.

Dit huis staat in een wijngaard en vervult de wens van de eigenaar op het platteland te wonen.

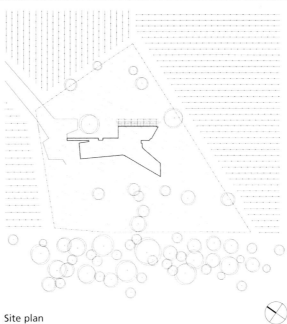

Site plan

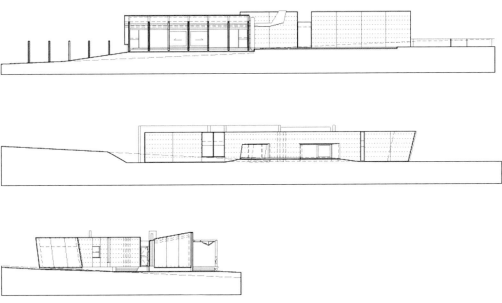

Elevations

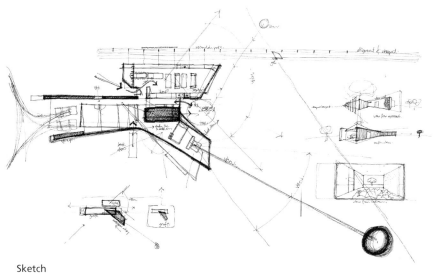

Sketch

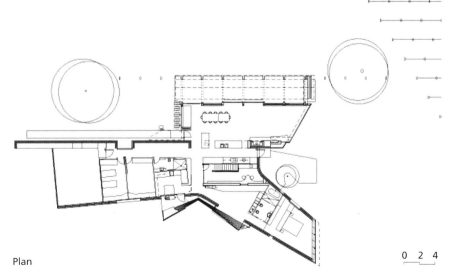

Plan

0 2 4

SURVEYING THE HORIZON

Conceição Macedo, Dante Macedo/Arquiprojecta

Santarem, Portugal | 2004
Photographs © Fernando Guerra/FG+SG

Die ungezähmte Natur der Ribatejo-Region liegt weit entfernt von den touristisch erschlossenen Gegenden Portugals. Der Minimalismus der natürlichen Umgebung wird durch den Grundriss und die schlichten Formen des Projekts noch verstärkt.

The wild, natural countryside of the Ribatejo region is far removed from the typical tourist spots of Portugal. The layout of this space and its shapes reinforce the concept of the home's minimal lines and horizontality.

La région sauvage de Ribatejo est bien loin des lieux touristiques du Portugal. Cette maison horizontale aux lignes épurées tire son caractère de l'agencement de l'espace et de sa forme.

De wilde natuur in de Ribetajo-streek is ver verwijderd van de typische toeristische plekken in Portugal. De indeling en de vormen van de ruimte versterken het concept van de minimale lijnen en de horizontale uitstraling van het huis.

Ein Gefühl von Ruhe und Frieden entsteht bei der Betrachtung der umliegenden Landschaft.

The local countryside transmits a feeling of peace.

Le paysage de cette région confère une impression de paix.

Het platteland in deze omgeving ademt een vredige sfeer.

Ground floor

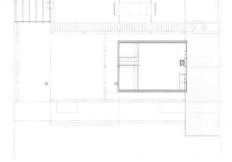

Mezzanine

0 2 4

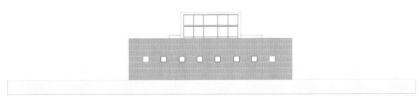

North elevation

East elevation

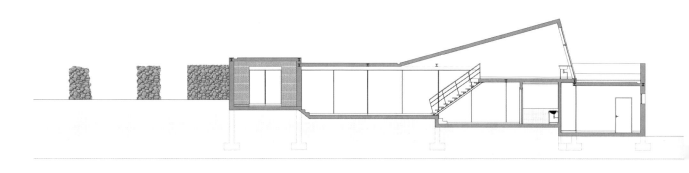

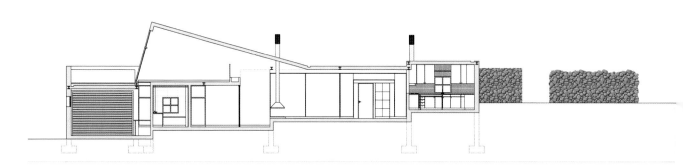

Longitudinal sections

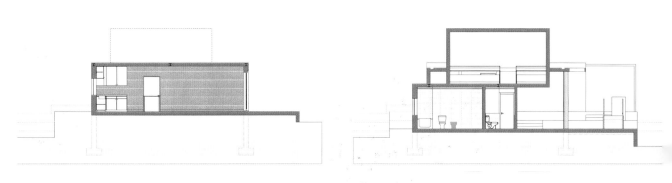

Cross sections

146

MATAJA RESIDENCE

Belzberg Architects

Malibu, CA, U.S.A. | 1999
Photographs © Tim Street-Porter

Das Design der Einzelbauten und die Einteilung des Grundrisses wurden von dem felsigen Untergrund maßgeblich beeinflusst. Ursprüngliches Ziel des Projektes war die Gestaltung eines weitab von der Hektik des Großstadtlebens gelegenen Rückzugsortes für die ganze Familie.

The rocks on the ground where this residence was built had a profound effect on the design of the various spaces and organization of the home. The initial objectives were to design a structure for a complete family home and build a bolthole to escape from the bustle of city life.

Les rochers sur lesquels l'habitation a été construite ont influencé l'aménagement et l'organisation des différentes pièces. L'objectif était de réaliser une maison familiale, tenant lieu de refuge loin de l'agitation de la ville.

De rotsen op de grond waar deze woning werd gebouwd, waren zeer bepalend voor het ontwerp van de diverse ruimten en de indeling van het huis. De begindoelstelling was een volledige gezinswoning te bouwen, een schuilplaats om het drukke stadsleven te ontvluchten.

Das Gebäude fügt sich ganz natürlich in die durch Felsformationen geprägte Landschaft ein.

The spaces are sited among rock formations and blend naturally in with the countryside.

Les espaces de plain-pied se fondent naturellement parmi les rochers.

De vertrekken liggen tussen rotsformaties en gaan op natuurlijke wijze in de omgeving op.

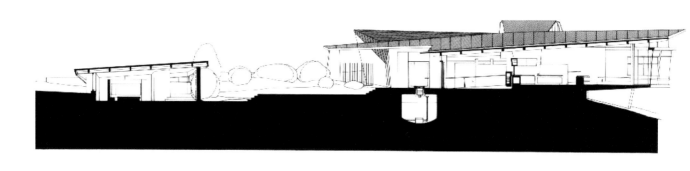

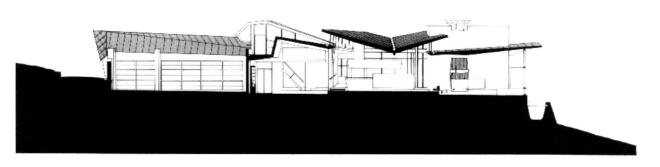

Sections

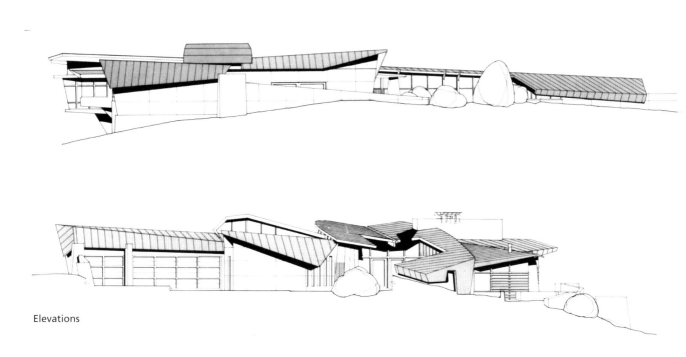

Elevations

150

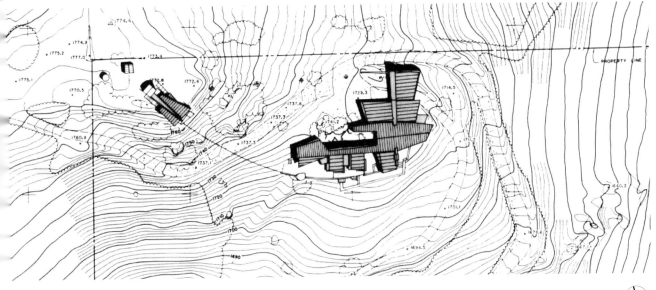

Site plan

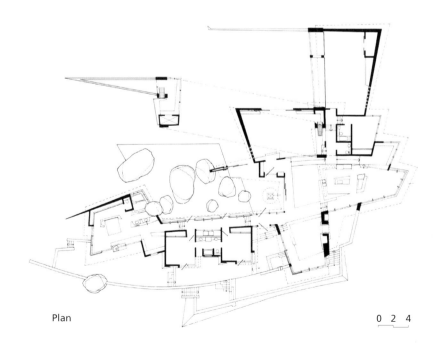

Plan   0 2 4

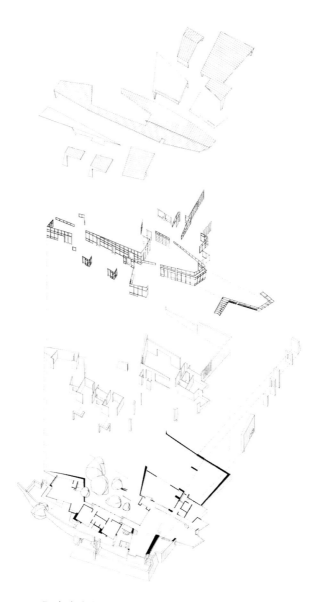

Exploded view

HOUSE IN RIGI SCHEIDEGG

Andreas Fuhrimann Gabrielle Hächler Architekten

Rigi Scheidegg, Switzerland | 2003
Photographs © Valentin Jeck

Das Wohnhaus wurde an den äußersten Rand des Grundstückes positioniert, um die größtmögliche Entfernung von den Nachbargrundstücken sowie den Bau eines zweiten Hauses zu ermöglichen. Es befindet sich nahe des zwischen Vierwaldstätter- und Zugsee gelegenen Rigi-Bergmassivs.

The house has been built on the edge of the property to increase the distance from neighboring houses and to leave open the option of building a second home in the future. The villages in this region are situated next to Mount Rigi, between the Four Cantons Lakes and Lake Zug.

La maison a été bâtie à la limite du terrain afin d'augmenter la distance la séparant des constructions voisines. Cela permet aussi d'édifier plus tard un second bâtiment. Les villages les plus proches se trouvent près du Mont Rigi, entre les lacs des Quatre-Cantons et de Zoug.

Dit huis is gebouwd aan de rand van het perceel, om de afstand tot angrenzende huizen zo groot mogelijk te maken en er later eventueel een tweede huis te bouwen. De dorpen in deze streek liggen dicht bij de Rigiberg, tussen het Vierwoudstrekenmeer en het Zugmeer.

Aus der erhöhten Lage des Ferienhauses genießt man den Panoramablick auf die Berge.

The residence stands on an elevated spot providing panoramic views of the mountains.

Cette habitation sur les hauteurs offre une splendide vue panoramique sur les montagnes.

De woning staat op een verhoogde plek, waar ze een weids uitzicht over de bergen heeft.

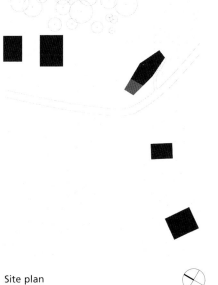

Site plan

Basement

Ground floor

First floor

0   2   4

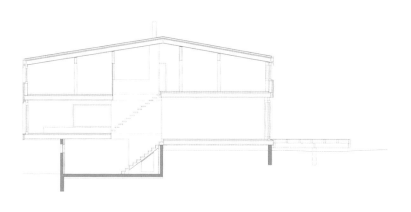

Section

SCHMUCK HOUSE

Hans Gangoly

Graz, Austria | 2005
Photographs © Paul Ott

Die auf einem starken Gefälle situierte Konstruktion scheint in der Luft zu schweben. Um die variierende Höhe des Grundstücks auszugleichen, ruhen Teile des Gebäudes auf Pfeilern. Eine von zwei Betonplatten gehaltene Fläche bildet das Fundament des 150 m² großen Wohnhauses.

This home, a construction that seems to be hanging in the air, stands on a fairly steep slope. To resolve the difference in levels, pillars have been used to support the structure. This 1,600 sq ft house consists essentially of a surface placed between two projecting concrete slabs facing east.

Semblant flotter dans les airs, cette maison de 150 m² est située sur une pente assez abrupte, tournée vers l'est. Afin de résoudre les différences de niveaux, on a utilisé des colonnes pour maintenir la structure.

Dit huis, dat in de lucht lijkt te hangen, staat op een tamelijk steile helling. Om het hoogteverschil op te lossen, ondersteunen pilaren het bouwwerk. Dit huis van 150 m² bestaat overwegend uit een vlak dat tussen twee uitstekende, op het oosten gerichte betonplaten is geplaatst.

Schmale Pfeiler stützen das Gebäude und geben ihm gleichzeitig ein graziles Aussehen.

Narrow pillars support and provide lightness to the structure.

De fines colonnes soutiennent la structure et lui donnent de la légèreté.

De slanke steunpilaren verlenen het bouwwerk lichtheid.

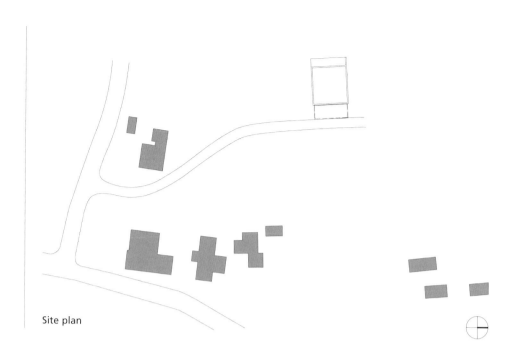

Site plan

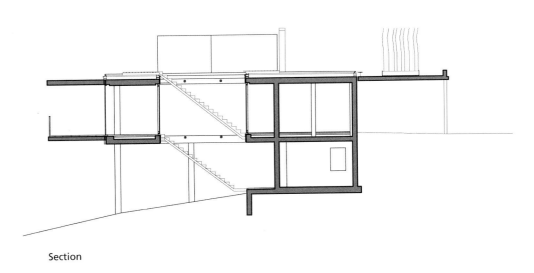

Section

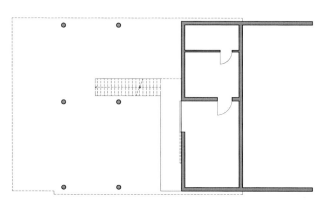

Basement

Ground floor

0 1

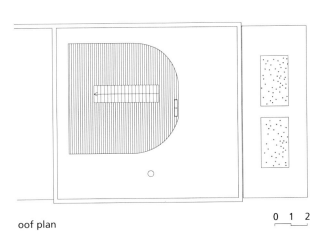

oof plan

0 1 2

HOUSE IN THE SIERRA DE ARRÁBIDA

Eduardo Souto de Moura

Sierra de Arrábida, Portugal | 2002
Photographs © Luís Ferreira Alves

Das Wohnhaus befindet sich auf einem unebenen Grundstück in der Sierra de Arrábida, einem Naturpark nahe Lissabon. Die schlichten, gradlinigen Bestandteile des Gebäudes umgeben einen großzügigen, zwischen Nord und Südfassade gelegenen Innenhof.

This home is situated in a spot of uneven topography in the Sierra de Arrábida, a natural park relatively near Lisbon. The house is made up of various simple, straight-edged structures, surrounding a spacious interior patio between the north and west facades.

La maison est située sur un terrain à la topographie accidentée, dans la Sierra de Arrábida, une réserve naturelle non loin de Lisbonne. Elle est composée de structures simples et variées, aux arêtes nettes, entourant un large patio entre ses façades nord et ouest.

Het huis staat op onregelmatig terrein in de Sierra de Arrábida, een natuurpark tamelijk dicht bij Lissabon. Het huis is opgebouwd uit een aantal eenvoudige, rechthoekige structuren die een ruime patio tussen de noordelijke en westelijke gevel omgeven.

Das Design des Wohnhauses entspricht dem typischen Stil des Architekten Souto de Moura.

This residence is typical of the architecture of its designer, Souto de Moura.

Cette demeure est typique de l'architecture de son concepteur, Eduardo Souto de Moura.

Deze woning is typerend voor de architectuur van de ontwerper, Souto de Moura.

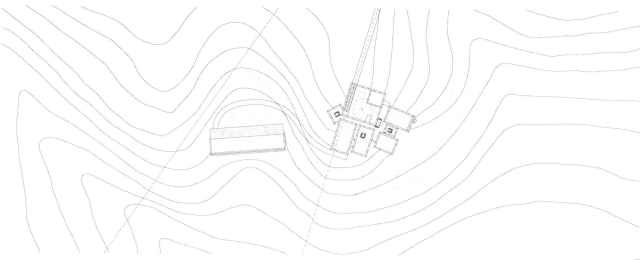

Site plan

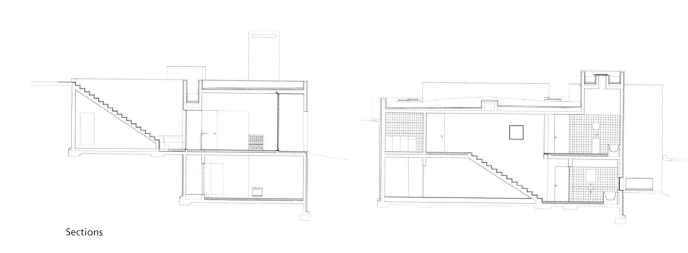

Sections

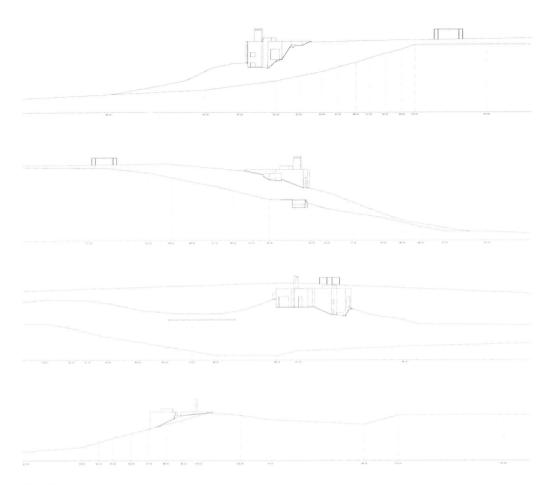

Elevations

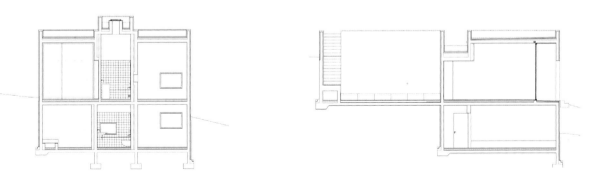

Sections

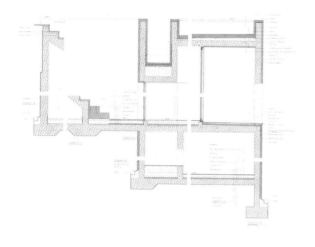

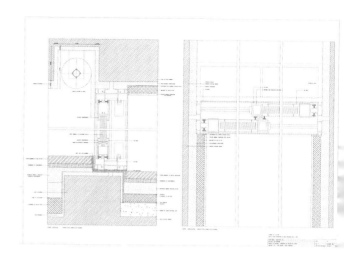

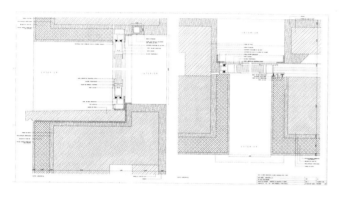

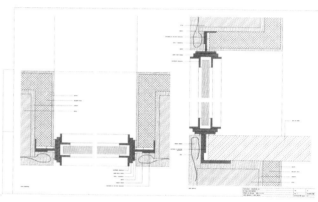

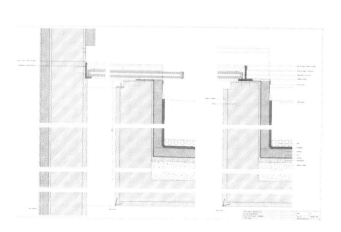

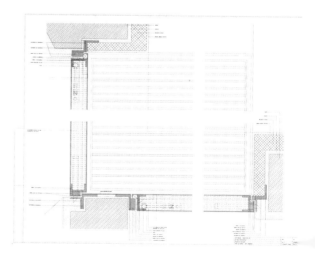

Construction details

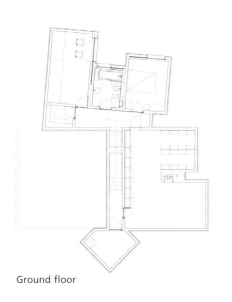

Ground floor

First floor

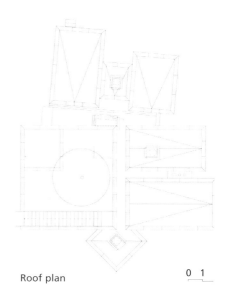

Roof plan

0 1

ROOFTECTURE S

Shuhei Endo Architect Institute

Kobe-city, Hyogo Prefecture, Japan | 2005
Photographs © Yoshiharu Matsumura

Auch bei diesem Projekt, das von einem Paar in Auftrag gegeben wurde, stellte der steile Abhang eine architektonische Herausforderung dar. Das wie ein längliches Dreieck geformte Grundstück ist knapp 20 Meter lang und hat eine Breite von 1,5 bis vier Metern.

The eternal issue of mixing slopes with architecture is addressed once again in this project, a small house which Shuhei Endo's firm, Paramodern, built for a couple. The lot is in the shape of an elongated triangle, some 65 feet long, with a depth of between 5 and 13 feet.

L'éternelle difficulté de concilier relief et architecture s'est à nouveau manifestée dans ce projet, une petite maison que le cabinet de Shuhei Endo, Paramodern, a créé pour un couple. Le terrain a la forme d'un triangle allongé, d'environ 20 m de long et d'une profondeur allant de 1,5 à 4 m.

Bij dit project werd de eeuwige uitdaging van het bouwen op een helling aangegaan. Het resultaat is een klein huis dat Paramodern, de onderneming van Shuhei Endo, voor een stel bouwde. Het perceel heeft de vorm van een aanggerekte driehoek van zo'n 20 meter lengte en 1,5 tot 4 meter breedte.

Das kleine Haus lehnt sich an eine Klippe über Japans Binnenmeer, der Seto-Inlandsee.

This small home stands up against an escarpment facing Setonaikai, Japan's inland sea.

Cette petite maison se tient sur une falaise face à Seto-Naikai, la mer intérieure du Japon.

Dit kleine huis rijst op tegen een steile helling die uitziet op Setonaikai, de Japanse Binnenzee.

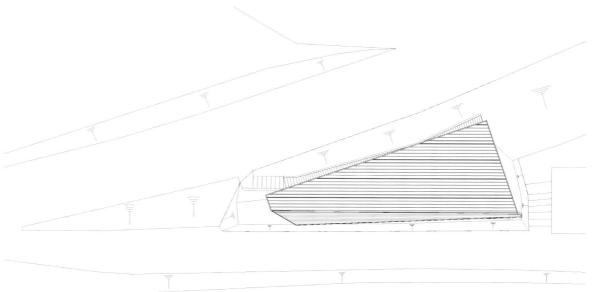

Site plan

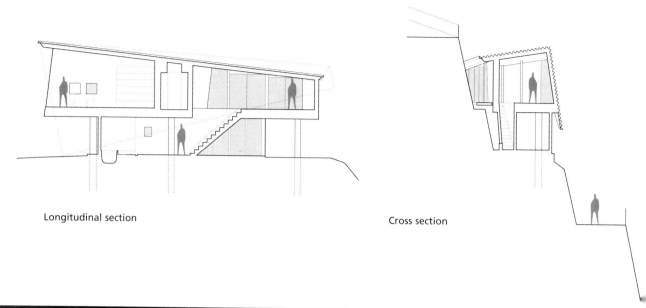

Longitudinal section

Cross section

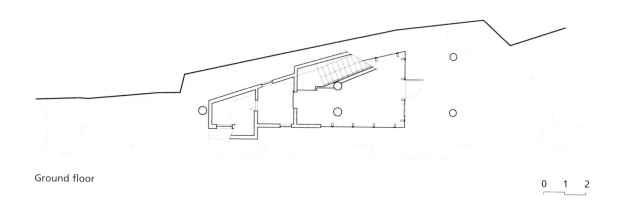

Ground floor

0 1 2

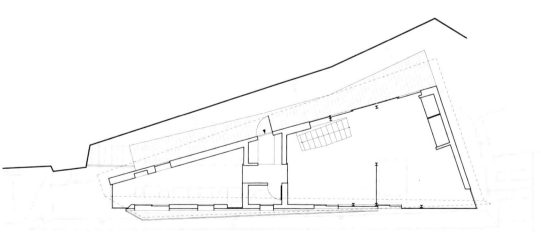

First floor

0   1   2

OS HOUSE

Nolaster

Loredo, Cantabria, Spain | 2005
Photographs © José Hevia

Zwischen Bilbao und Santander liegen einige Ortschaften, die mögliche Wohnorte für Stadtmenschen darstellen. Mit dem äußeren Erscheinungsbild, der Bauweise und den Materialien der „Casa Os" wird das Ziel verfolgt, einen potenziellen Erstwohnsitz zu errichten.

Some communities in between Bilbao and Santander are potential places to live for city folks. The Os House aims to act as the definition of a first home in a superurban structure, and the decisions taken regarding the appearance, presence and construction materials reflect this.

Certaines communes entre Bilbao et Santander sont susceptibles de devenir des lieux d'habitation pour les citadins. La maison Os vise à servir de référence pour une première résidence « superurbaine ». Les choix esthétiques, la situation et les matériaux utilisés reflètent cette démarche.

Sommige dorpjes tussen Bilbao en Santander vormen een geschikte woonplaats voor stadsmensen. Huis Os wil de definitie zijn van een eerste huis in een typisch bouwwerk. Het uiterlijk, de mate van aanwezigheid in de omgeving en de bouwmaterialen weerspiegelen deze wens.

Eine ideale Lösung für zwischen Stadt und Land gelegene Häuser bildet dieses Konzept.

The architects have presented an idea for homes between the urban and rural environments.

Les architectes ont présenté une idée de maison à mi-chemin entre l'urbain et le rural.

De architecten vonden een concept voor huizen met een half-stedelijke en half-landelijke ligging.

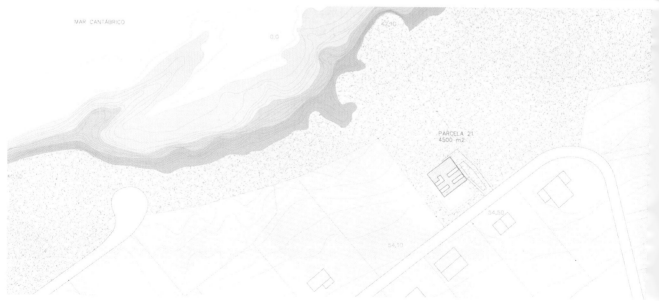

Site plan

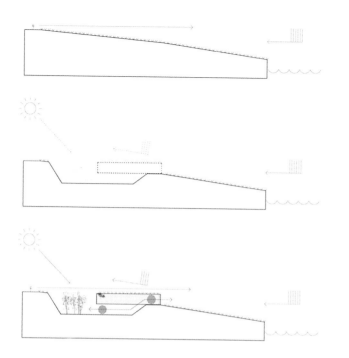
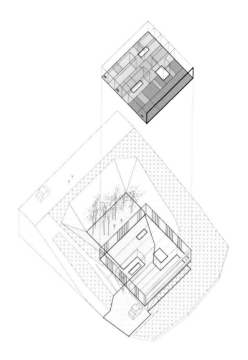

Conceptual diagrams

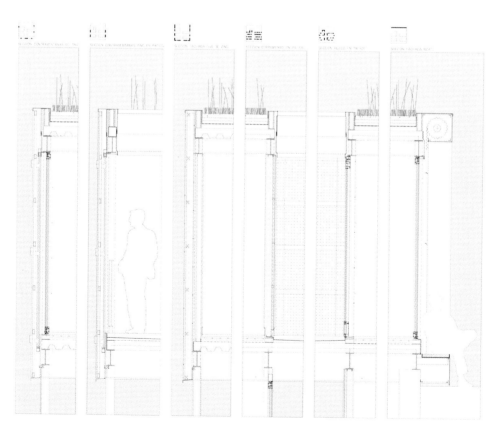

Sections

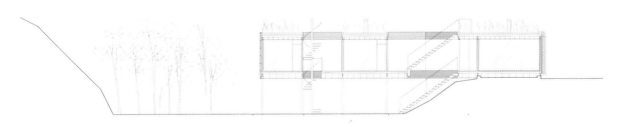

Section

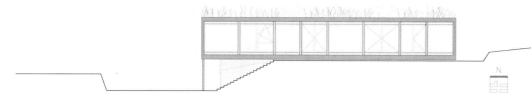

North elevation

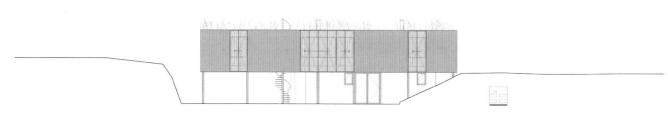

South elevation

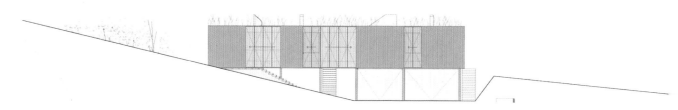

East elevation

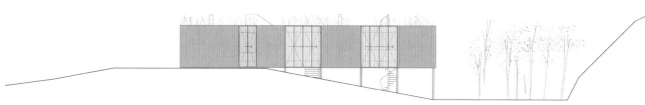

West elevation

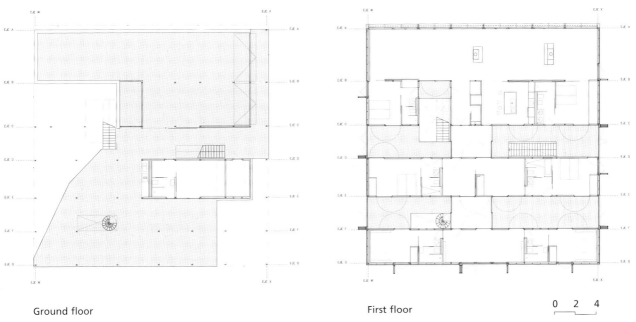

Ground floor

First floor

0 2 4

BRICKELL-POLLOCK HOUSE

Hopkinson Team Architecture

Bethells Beach, New Zealand | 2004
Photographs © Simon Devitt

Hier wird beispielhaft aufgezeigt, wie aus einem einfachen Gebäude eine unvergleichliche Kulisse entstehen kann. Bei dem am Bethell's Beach an der Westküste der Insel gelegenen Ferienhaus bestimmt die Aussicht auf den Tasmanischen See und den Kanukawald Ausrichtung und Struktur des Hauses.

This is an example of how to blend a simple building into an outstanding setting. The holiday home is located at Bethell's Beach region, on the west coast of the North Island where views of the Tasman Sea and the Kanuka forest determine the house's orientation and the layout of its structures.

Cette maison de vacances est située dans la région de Bethell's Beach, sur la côte ouest de l'île du Nord, où la vue sur la mer de Tasmanie et la forêt Kanuka détermine l'orientation et l'agencement des constructions.C'est un parfait exemple d'harmonie entre une habitation et un lieu exceptionnel.

Hier is te zien hoe een eenvoudig bouwwerk één wordt met een markante omgeving. Het vakantiehuis staat in de streek van Bethell's Beach aan de westkust van het noordelijke eiland. De ligging en vormgeving ervan worden bepaald door het uitzicht over de Tasmanzee en het kanukawoud.

Dieses Wohnhaus eröffnet eine beeindruckende Aussicht auf den Tasmanischen See.

This residence is on top of a hill, with stunning views of the valley and the Tasman Sea.

Située en haut d'une colline, cette villa offre une vue splendide sur la vallée et la mer de Tasmanie.

Deze woning staat op een heuvel en kijkt prachtig uit over de Tasmanzee en -vallei.

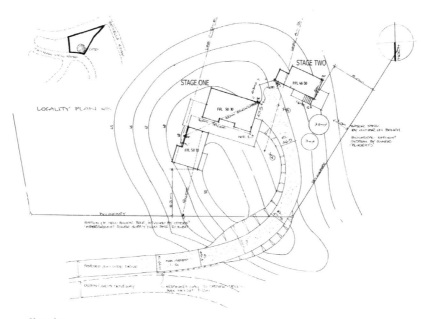

Site plan

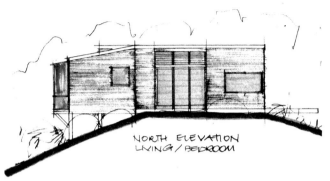

North elevation

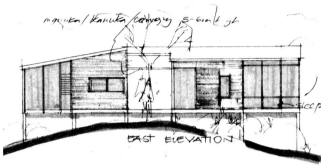

East elevation

North elevation studio

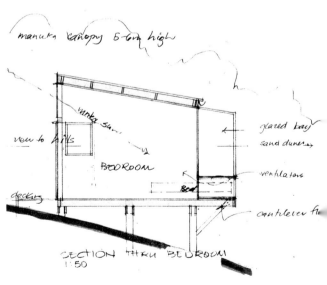

Section

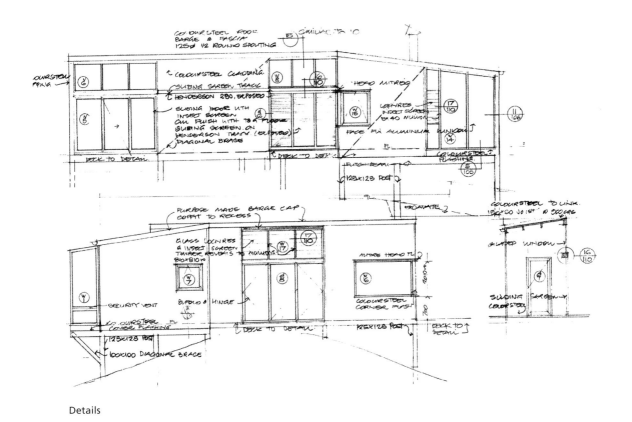

Details

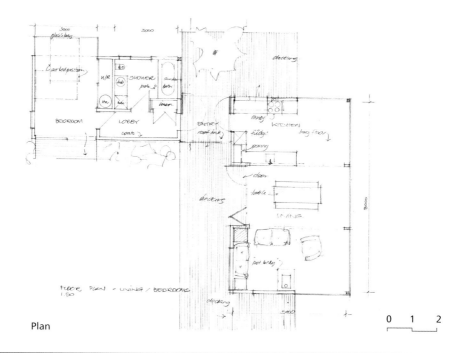

Plan

0 1 2

DOWNING RESIDENCE

Ibarra Rosano Design Architects

Tucson, AZ, U.S.A. | 2003
Photographs © Bill Timmerman

Die hohen Kakteen und die dichte Pflanzendecke des Grundstücks wurden beibehalten, um das Gebäude mit der Kulisse harmonieren zu lassen. Gläserne überdachte Übergänge verbinden die drei Einzelbauten, sodass der Ausblick auf die umliegende Landschaft nicht versperrt wird.

The pavilions making up this residence have been distributed among the tall cacti and dense vegetation areas that formerly occupied the lot and which have been kept to adapt the house to the setting. The three structures are joined by glass breezeways in order to capture the best views.

C'est la maison qui s'adapte à son environnement : les différents pavillons ont été répartis parmi les hauts cactus et les zones de végétation dense qui recouvraient le terrain. Les trois bâtiments communiquent par des galeries en verre permettant d'apprécier la vue.

De paviljoenen waaruit dit huis is opgebouwd, liggen verspreid tussen grote cactussen en dichte vegetatie. Deze begroeiing is behouden om het huis in de omgeving te laten opgaan. De drie elementen zijn met elkaar verbonden via passages van glas, voor een zo groot mogelijk uitzicht.

Die drei das Gesamthaus bildenden Bauten wurden inmitten einer Saguaro-Kakteen-Landschaft errichtet.

The three volumes of the home are gently situated among groups of saguaro cactus.

Les trois volumes de cette résidence sont délicatement posés parmi les cactus saguaro.

De drie elementen van het huis zijn vriendelijk gelegen tussen groepjes reuzencactussen.

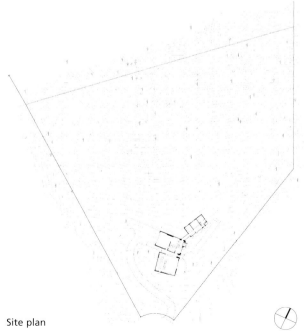

Site plan

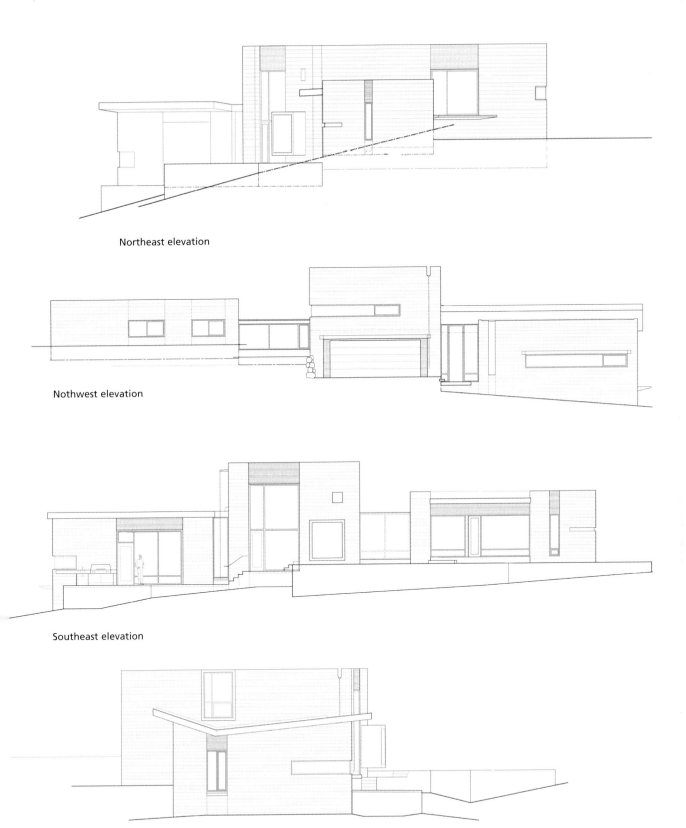

Northeast elevation

Nothwest elevation

Southeast elevation

Southwest elevation

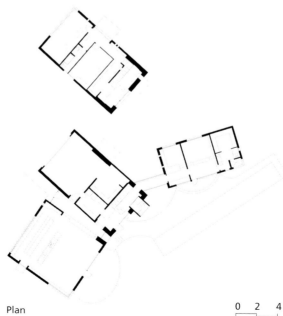

Plan

0   2   4

LAVAFLOW 2

Craig Steely

Big Island, HI, U.S.A. | 2004
Photographs © JD Peterson

Beim Entwurf des Gebäudes achtete der Architekt darauf, die einmalige Landschaft – eine Vulkaninsel auf Hawaii – unberührt zu lassen. Tagsüber kann die vom Krater steigende Rauchsäule betrachtet werden, während der Feuerschein des Vulkaninneren den Nachthimmel erleuchtet.

The architect has designed a home that does not transform the lot it stands on, a volcanic area on the Big Island of Hawaii. The landscape is unique; by day one can see a column of smoke emerging from the crater and at night, the glare of the volcano's furnace is reflected in the clouds.

L'architecte a conçu une maison qui ne transforme pas le terrain sur lequel elle est bâtie, dans une région volcanique de la Grande Île d'Hawaii. Le paysage est unique ; de jour, on voit la fumée s'échapper en colonne du cratère et, la nuit, la lave incandescente du volcan se reflète dans les nuages.

De architect heeft een huis ontworpen dat de omgeving waar het staat, vulkanisch gebied op het Grote Eiland van Hawaii, niet aantast. Het landschap is uniek. Overdag is een rookkolom boven de krater zichtbaar en 's nachts wordt de gloed van de vulkaanoven in de wolken weerspiegeld.

Bei einer derart sensiblen Umgebung muss nachhaltiges Design Priorität genießen.

In these precarious surroundings, the sustainability of the design is essential.

Dans cet environnement incertain, la résistance de la construction est essentielle.

Op deze risicovolle plek is het essentieel dat het ontwerp tegen de omgeving bestand is.

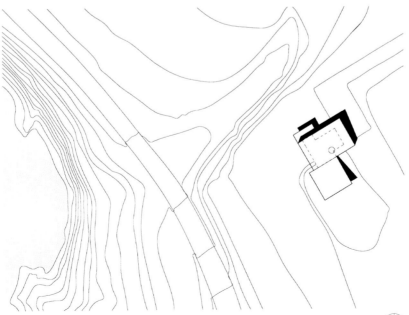

Site plan

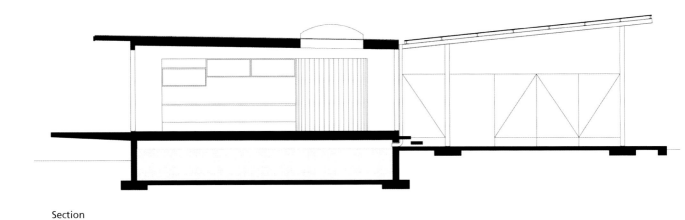

Section

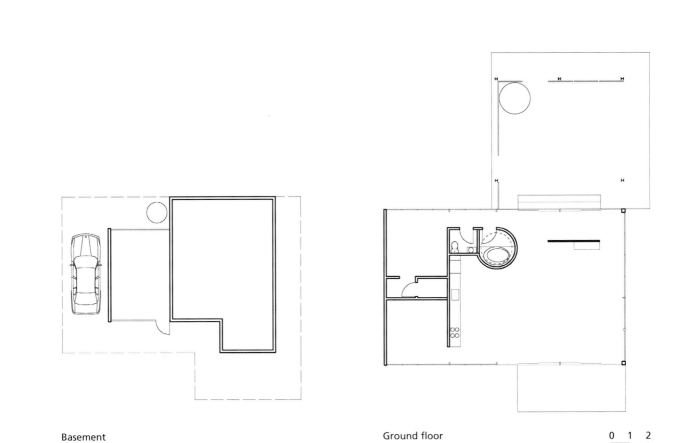

Basement

Ground floor

0 1 2

JENNINGS RESIDENCE

Workroom Design

Hopkins Point, Warrnambool, Australia | 2002
Photographs © Trevor Mein/Meinphoto

Das an der Südküste Australiens gelegene Haus wurde in direkter Nähe einer Klippe am Indischen Ozean errichtet. Selbst in der günstigsten Jahreszeit ist das Klima in dieser Gegend rau. Während der Entwurfsphase wurden besonders der felsige Baugrund und der herrliche Ausblick berücksichtigt.

This residence stands 50 yards from the edge of a cliff overlooking the Indian Ocean, on the south coast of Australia. The climate of this region is extreme; even in good conditions it is harsh. The rocky ground and the incredible views were the features taken into consideration at the design stage.

Cette résidence se situe à 45 mètres d'une falaise surplombant l'océan Indien, sur la côte sud de l'Australie. Le sol rocheux, les vues incroyables et les contraintes climatiques ont influencé la conception du projet.

Deze woning ligt zo'n 45 meter van de rand van een klif met uitzicht op de Indische Oceaan, aan de zuidkust van Australië. De streek heeft een extreem klimaat, dat eigenlijk altijd erg onvriendelijk is. Bij het ontwerp werd rekening gehouden met de rotsachtige grond en het uitzicht.

Bei der Ausrichtung des Gebäudes spielte die Landschaft eine maßgebliche Rolle.

The land where this home stands has been the determining factor for its orientation.

La situation du terrain a été un facteur déterminant de l'orientation de la maison.

De grond waar dit huis op staat, is bepalend geweest voor zijn ligging.

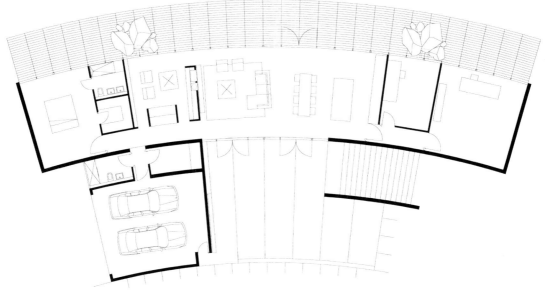

Floor plan

0 1 2

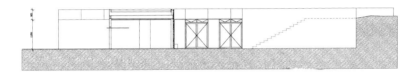

North elevation

South elevation

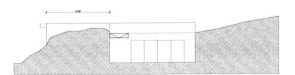

East elevation

West elevation

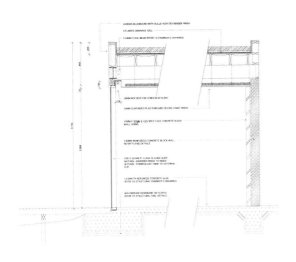

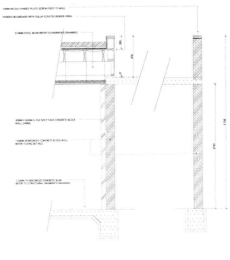

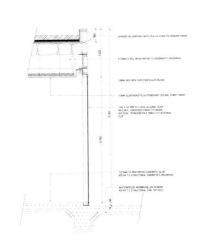

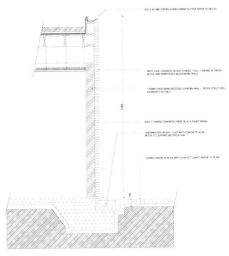

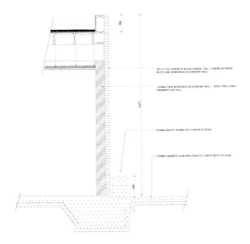

Construction details

RESIDENCE IN DALAAS

Gohm & Hiessberger

Dalaas, Austria | 2005
Photographs © Bruno Klomfar

ine Herausforderung bei der Konstruktion des Hauses stellte der steile Hang
ar. Auch wenn es durch moderne Linien und Extravaganz charakterisiert ist,
igt sich das Gebäude dank regelmäßiger, klarer Formen optimal in die
andschaft und die regionaltypische Architektur ein.

his home has managed to make the most of its location, on a steep slope;
nd although its design is highly contemporary and original, the building
ends in perfectly with the surroundings and with the rest of the homes in
e area thanks to its regular, defined shapes, such as its gabled roof.

ette maison a brillamment tiré parti de son emplacement sur une pente
ide. Bien qu'elle soit originale, elle se fond parfaitement dans son cadre
aturel et s'harmonise avec les habitations voisines grâce à ses lignes
gulières et bien définies, comme son toit à pignon.

t huis is erin geslaagd zijn omgeving, een steile helling, optimaal te
enutten. Hoewel het ontwerp erg hedendaags en origineel is, past het
ebouw zich volmaakt aan de omgeving en de overige huizen in het gebied
n, dankzij de regelmatige, uitgesproken vormen, zoals het puntdak.

**Die Berglandschaft der Österreichischen Alpen
liefert den Standort des Einfamilienhauses.**

**The house is situated in a mountainous area in
the Austrian Alps.**

**Ce « chalet » est situé dans les Alpes
autrichiennes.**

**Het huis is gelegen in een bergachtig gebied in
de Oostenrijkse Alpen.**

Site plan

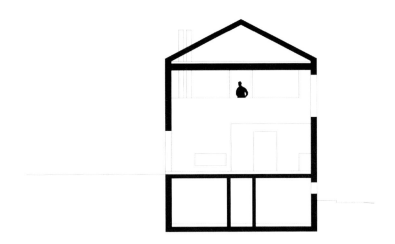

Section

North elevation

South elevation

East elevation

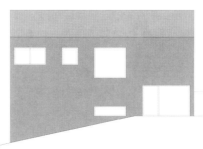

West elevation

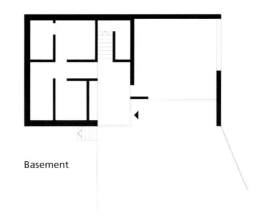

Basement

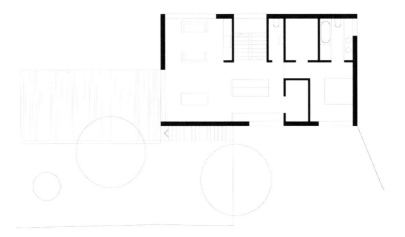

Ground floor

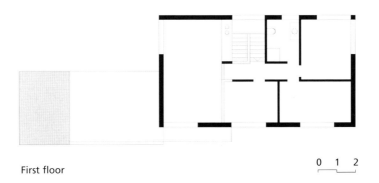

First floor

0 1 2

HOUSE IN ANAPOIMA

Guillermo Arias, Luis Cuartas

Anapoima, Colombia | 2006
Photographs © Carlos Tobón

Der nahe bei Bogotá gelegene Wochenendsitz befindet sich in der Region der Mesa de Yuegas, etwa 700 Meter über dem Meeresspiegel. Aufgrund der großartigen Aussicht auf die Berge wurde ein offener Grundriss gewählt, der den direkten Kontakt zur Umgebung ermöglicht.

This weekend home is just over 40 miles from Bogotá, in the Mesa de Yeguas region, 2,300 feet above sea level. The lot faces a gully and has amazing views of the mountains. These features advocated the design of an open-plan home, in direct contact with the natural landscape.

Idéale pour le week-end, cette maison est à 65 km de Bogotá, dans la région de Mesa de Yeguas, à 700 m au-dessus du niveau de la mer. L'architecte a choisi une conception ouverte, avec un contact direct avec la nature, car le terrain domine un ravin et offre une vue spectaculaire sur les montagnes.

Dit vakantiehuis ligt op zo'n 65 kilometer afstand van Bogotá in de regio van de Mesa de Yeguas, 700 meter boven dee zeespiegel. De loft ziet uit op een vallei en over de bergen. Daarom werd gekozen voor een open ontwerp dat direct in contact staat met de omgeving.

Die eindrucksvolle Natur und das angenehme Klima machen das Wohnen zu einem Vergnügen.

The stunning landscape and magnificent climate are features that favor this home the most.

Son paysage unique et le climat idéal sont les atouts les plus appréciés de cette maison.

Door het fraaie landschap en het mooie klimaat komt dit huis erg goed tot zijn recht.

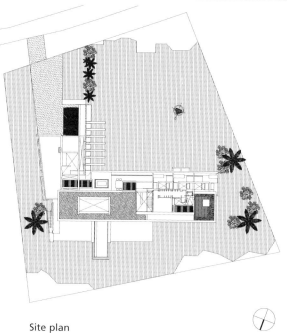

Site plan

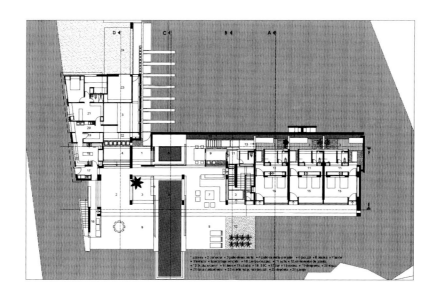

Ground floor

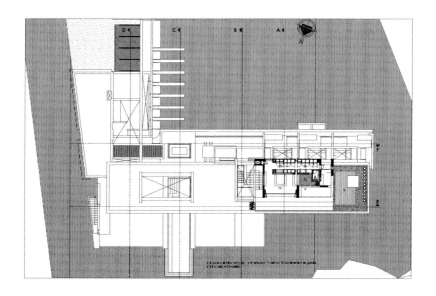

First floor

0   2   4

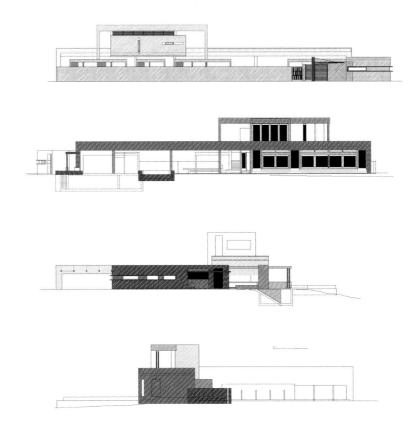

Elevations

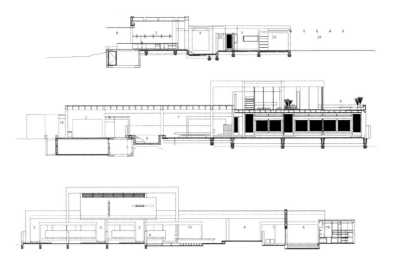

Sections